The Corporate Guide

To the Universe with AI

Akashni Ashok Latchanna

DEDICATION

This book is dedicated to the insatiable curiosity of human kind.

CONTENTS

ACKNOWLEDGMENTS

To the brilliant minds of innovators, scientists, and mathematicians across the globe—your unwavering curiosity, relentless pursuit of knowledge, and groundbreaking discoveries have not only pushed the boundaries of human understanding but have also laid the foundation for a future filled with endless possibilities. Your work, often carried out in the quiet of laboratories, under the vast canopy of the night sky, or within the silent confines of theory, serves as a beacon of hope and progress. From the smallest subatomic particles to the vast expanse of the universe, from the elegant simplicity of numbers to the complex algorithms driving our digital world, you map the unknown, turn dreams into reality, and forge paths where none existed. Let this be an acknowledgment of your invaluable contributions to humanity and an inspiration for future generations to continue exploring, questioning, and innovating. Your legacy is the light that guides us forward.

Introduction: Steering Through the Corporate Cosmos with AI

In the corporate universe, businesses navigate through a constellation of challenges, from data nebulae obscuring clear decision paths to communication black holes swallowing up vital information. Sometimes you're just thrown with heads, managers and that one co-worker that posesses black holes for souls. Irrespective the challenges, in this cosmic complexity, Artificial Intelligence (AI) has emerged to help businesses – or employees with idiot bosses - cut out time consuming work to focus on what matters.

Purpose of the Book

"Navigating the Universe with AI" embarks on an exploratory mission to decipher how AI technologies are revolutionizing corporates, transforming obstacles into opportunities, and streamlining the workflows that propel businesses forward. Our journey is guided by a seemingly unremarkable yet pivotal figure: the office worker with a laptop. This character, equipped with AI tools, symbolizes the bridge between human intuition and the raw computational power of AI. Together, they form a formidable duo capable of traversing the corporate cosmos more efficiently than ever before.

This book is not just a map of the territory but a blueprint for constructing the future. My aim is to demystify AI for business leaders, managers, and workers alike, demonstrating practical ways AI can be harnessed to tackle real-world business challenges. By weaving through case studies, theoretical insights, and speculative futures, we will uncover the multifaceted roles AI plays in enhancing productivity, fostering innovation, and creating value.

Our central metaphor—the "corporate universe"—reflects the modern business environment. Companies orbit around their core missions, propelled by the gravitational forces of market demands and competitive pressures. AI acts as a navigational aid, helping businesses avoid the asteroids of disruption and reach new frontiers of growth and efficiency.

As we chart this course, we also confront the myths and misconceptions surrounding AI. Far from the cold, impersonal machines of science fiction, the AI tools of today are increasingly sophisticated, capable of augmenting human creativity and empathy with unprecedented analytical and processing capabilities. Our guide, we'll name him Bob, symbolizes this synergy—harnessing the power of AI to solve problems, make informed decisions, and connect with customers and colleagues in more meaningful ways.

The Evolution of AI in Business

The odyssey of AI from academic laboratories to the heart of global commerce is a testament to human ingenuity and the relentless pursuit of innovation. The seeds of AI were planted in the mid-20th century, germinating in the fertile soil of mathematics, computer science, and engineering. These early efforts aimed to create machines that could mimic human intelligence, a quest that has evolved into the development of systems capable of learning, adapting, and working alongside us.

In the 1980s and 1990s, AI experienced its first waves of commercial application, from rudimentary expert systems to the initial forays into machine learning. However, it was the explosion of data and computational power in the 21st century that truly ignited the AI revolution. Today, AI permeates every sector, from finance and healthcare to retail and manufacturing, driving efficiencies and enabling innovations that were previously unimaginable.

Key milestones in AI's evolution have been marked by breakthroughs such as IBM's Deep Blue defeating world chess champion Garry Kasparov in 1997, a symbol of AI's potential to outthink humans in specific domains. In 2011, IBM's Watson triumphed on the quiz show Jeopardy!, showcasing the ability of AI to understand and process natural language. More recently, the development of generative AI models has opened new horizons for creative and analytical tasks, from designing products to optimizing supply chains.

These technological breakthroughs are not just technical achievements; they represent a paradigm shift in how businesses operate and compete. AI technologies, powered by advancements in machine learning, natural language processing, and robotics, offer unprecedented insights into market trends, customer preferences, and operational efficiencies. They have become indispensable tools for decision-makers, providing a competitive edge in a rapidly changing corporate landscape.

Yet, the journey of AI in business is not without its challenges. Concerns about privacy, ethics, and the displacement of jobs have sparked important conversations about the responsible use of AI. Businesses are learning that the successful integration of AI requires not just technical skill but a thoughtful approach that balances innovation with humanity, ethics with ambition.

"Navigating the Universe with AI" aims to be a compass for this journey, guiding readers through the complexities of implementing and benefiting from AI in business. Our exploration will take us beyond the hype, diving deep into the practicalities of AI adoption, the strategies for overcoming obstacles, and the principles for ethical use. Through the lens of our guiding character, we will witness firsthand the transformative power of AI—making the vast corporate universe not only navigable but ripe with possibilities.

As we set sail on this adventure, our goal is to inspire, inform, and empower. Whether you are a business leader steering your organization into new territories, a manager seeking to optimize your team's workflow, or an employee navigating the changing landscape of your industry, AI offers tools and insights to help you chart your course. Together, we will discover how, with AI as our ally, we can navigate the corporate universe with greater agility, creativity, and foresight.

Welcome aboard "Navigating the Universe with AI." Let's embark on this journey together, exploring how the fusion of human intelligence and artificial ingenuity is not just shaping the future of business but also redefining what it means to work, innovate, and succeed in the cosmic dance of the corporate universe.

Part 1: Understanding the Corporate Universe

1 The Galaxy of Modern Business

IN THE BOUNDLESS EXPANSE of the universe, galaxies are vast and mesmerizing constructs, swirling with stars, planets, and myriad celestial phenomena, each following complex, intertwined paths through the cosmos. This cosmic dance, governed by the fundamental laws of physics, mirrors the equally intricate and dynamic realm of the modern corporate world. Here, companies of every size and from every sector orbit around their core missions, propelled and influenced by the gravitational forces of market demand, competition, and innovation. This chapter ventures into the heart of the corporate galaxy, exploring the phenomena of globalization, digital transformation, and the relentless pace of change that characterizes our era.

Navigating Through Complexity

The modern corporate environment is a complex system, a galaxy in its own right, where businesses navigate through a space teeming with opportunities and challenges. Just as celestial bodies are influenced by the gravitational forces within a galaxy, companies are driven and shaped by market dynamics, competitive pressures, and the constant push towards innovation. The brightness of a business, much like that of a star, is determined by its ability to harness these forces effectively, to innovate, and to outshine competitors.

This complexity is not a mere backdrop; it is an active, evolving force, shaped by technological advancements, market shifts, and changes in consumer behaviour. The intricate web of relationships between different sectors—technology, finance, healthcare, and retail, among others—creates a dynamic ecosystem where actions in one corner can send ripples across the entire galaxy. These interconnections can amplify risks but also open up vast opportunities for those who navigate them wisely.

Globalization: The Expansion into New Worlds

Globalization has stretched far beyond its traditional boundaries, making remote markets more accessible and weaving together the fates of economies across the planet. In this expanded field of play, businesses venture beyond their local domains, driven by the quest for new markets, resources, and talent. This global expansion mirrors the exploratory journeys of astronomers and adventurers, reaching into unknown spaces to uncover new opportunities and challenges.

The impact of globalization dissolves barriers, fosters an exchange of goods, ideas, and cultures, and introduces a level of diversity and interconnection that was unimaginable in past epochs. Companies can source materials from across the globe, tap into emerging markets with billions of potential customers, and build collaborative networks that span continents.

However, navigating this expanded galaxy is not without its perils. The global marketplace is a competitive arena where cultural nuances, regulatory landscapes, and economic fluctuations can dramatically affect the success of cross-border ventures. The same forces that open new opportunities also expose businesses to more complex risks, requiring them to be more adaptive, culturally aware, and strategically agile than ever before.

The Dawn of Digital Transformation

As significant as the impact of globalization has been the advent of digital transformation, reshaping the corporate galaxy at an unprecedented pace. Digital technologies—once mere tools for operational efficiency—have become the foundation upon which businesses build their strategies, interact with customers, and create value.

Digital transformation marks a shift as profound as the transition from sail to steam in the age of exploration. It has democratized information, decentralized decision-making, and disrupted traditional business models across every sector.

In the corporate galaxy, digital technologies act as accelerators, propelling businesses forward at speeds that were once unthinkable.

This transformation is characterized by the adoption of cloud computing, big data analytics, artificial intelligence, and the Internet of Things (IoT). These technologies enable businesses to navigate the vast data nebulae, uncovering insights that drive smarter decisions, streamline operations, and personalize customer experiences. In the digital realm, agility and the ability to innovate continuously are the keys to survival and success.

It becomes evident that the forces of globalization and digital transformation are not mere external pressures but catalysts for innovation and growth. These phenomena, while challenging, also present unparalleled opportunities for businesses willing to adapt and evolve.

The Gravity of Technology and Innovation

Technology and innovation serve as the gravity that holds systems together and propels them into new orbits. The rapid evolution of digital technologies has not only changed the way businesses operate but has redefined the very essence of what it means to be a company in the modern world.

This digital dawn has given birth to new business models that challenge traditional notions of commerce, collaboration, and competition. Platforms and ecosystems have emerged as powerful new forms of organization, where value is created not just within a single company but across networks of partners, suppliers, and customers. This shift mirrors the transition in astronomy from a geocentric to a heliocentric understanding of our solar system; just as the sun became recognized as the center around which planets orbit, so too have platforms and ecosystems become central to the creation of value in the digital age.

Navigating Digital Transformation

The journey through digital transformation is as varied as the celestial bodies that populate our universe. For some businesses, it involves a complete overhaul of legacy systems and processes; for others, it's a more gradual integration of digital technologies into existing operations. The common thread, however, is the need for a strategic vision that aligns technology with business objectives, fostering a culture of continuous innovation and adaptation.

This journey is fraught with challenges, from the technical hurdles of integrating new technologies to the cultural shifts required to embrace a digital-first mindset. Yet, the rewards for those who navigate this transformation successfully are immense. Digital technologies offer unprecedented levels of efficiency, agility, and customer insight, enabling businesses to move at the speed of light in response to changing market dynamics.

The Speed of Change

The pace of change has accelerated to near-light speed, driven by the relentless advance of technology and the global integration of markets. This rapid evolution can be disorienting, as businesses must constantly adapt to new technologies, competitive pressures, and shifting customer expectations.

In this environment, agility and resilience become paramount. Businesses must develop the capacity to pivot quickly in response to emerging trends and disruptions. This requires not only technological capability but also a culture that values learning, experimentation, and the ability to fail fast and learn faster.

Globalization Revisited: The Interstellar Web of Connectivity

As we dive deeper into the impact of globalization, it's clear that its influence extends beyond the mere expansion of markets. Globalization has woven an interstellar web of connectivity, linking economies, cultures, and businesses in a complex, interdependent network. This connectivity has facilitated the flow of ideas, talent, and capital across borders, sparking innovation and driving economic growth.

However, this interconnectedness also means that disturbances in one part of the corporate galaxy can have ripple effects throughout the system. Economic crises, geopolitical tensions, and environmental disasters in one region can impact supply chains, markets, and business operations globally. Navigating this web of connectivity requires a keen understanding of global dynamics and the ability to anticipate and respond to shifts in the international landscape.

The Future of the Corporate Galaxy

As we look to the horizon, the future appears both exciting and uncertain. Advances in AI, quantum computing, and biotechnology promise to unleash new waves of innovation, potentially transforming the way we live and work in ways we can scarcely imagine. At the same time, these technologies pose ethical dilemmas and societal challenges that businesses will need to navigate carefully.

In this ever-evolving galaxy, the role of leadership becomes crucial. Leaders must possess not only a visionary outlook but also the humility to listen and learn from every corner of their organizations and the ecosystems in which they operate. They must navigate their businesses with a clear moral compass, ensuring that the pursuit of innovation and growth is balanced with considerations of ethics, sustainability, and social responsibility.

The journey is an ongoing adventure, filled with challenges, opportunities, and the constant drive to explore new horizons. As businesses continue to navigate the forces of globalization and digital transformation, they will need to remain agile, innovative, and grounded in a strong sense of purpose.

The future of the corporate galaxy is not written in the stars but will be shaped by the choices we make today. By embracing change, fostering innovation, and adhering to ethical principles, businesses can not only survive but thrive in the vast, dynamic universe of modern commerce.

Embracing a Galactic Perspective

Businesses must adopt a galactic perspective. This means looking beyond immediate challenges and opportunities to understand the broader forces shaping the business landscape. It involves recognizing patterns in the market, anticipating shifts in consumer behaviour, and staying ahead of technological advancements. Like astronomers who study the movements of celestial bodies to understand the universe, business leaders must analyse market trends and data to guide their decision-making.

The Power of Data Navigation

In a galaxy where information is as vast as the stars, the ability to navigate through data becomes a critical skill. Big data and analytics offer businesses the telescopes and maps they need to chart their course. By harnessing the power of data, companies can gain insights into customer preferences, optimize their operations, and predict future trends. This data-driven approach enables businesses to make informed decisions, reduce risks, and identify new opportunities for growth.

However, navigating through data requires more than just sophisticated technology; it demands a culture that values data literacy and critical thinking. Businesses must invest in training and tools that empower employees across all levels to interpret data effectively and apply these insights to their work.

Adapting to the Pace of Technological Evolution

The velocity of technological change is relentless. To keep up, businesses must cultivate a culture of learning and innovation. This entails continuously exploring new technologies, experimenting with different approaches, and being willing to pivot when necessary.

Adaptability in the face of technological evolution also means being open to rethinking business models and processes. Companies that are flexible and agile can more easily integrate new technologies into their operations and quickly respond to market changes. This adaptability is a competitive advantage, enabling businesses to thrive in a rapidly evolving environment.

Sustainable Navigation: Ethical Considerations and Social Responsibility

As businesses chart their course, it's crucial to navigate with a sense of responsibility toward the planet and society. The pursuit of growth must be balanced with ethical considerations and a commitment to sustainability. This includes addressing the environmental impact of business operations, ensuring fair labor practices, and contributing positively to the communities in which companies operate.

Sustainable navigation also involves being mindful of the ethical implications of new technologies, particularly in areas such as AI and data privacy. By prioritizing ethical considerations and social responsibility, businesses can build trust with customers and stakeholders, fostering long-term loyalty and success.

The Role of Collaboration in Exploring New Frontiers

No business is an island. Collaboration and partnership are essential for exploring new frontiers and tackling the complex challenges of today's business environment. By working together, companies can share knowledge, resources, and risks, creating synergies that benefit all parties involved.

This collaborative spirit extends beyond traditional business partnerships to include collaboration with governments, non-profit organizations, and the broader community. Such alliances can drive innovation, address societal challenges, and create more sustainable and inclusive economic growth.

Looking to the Horizon

As we stand on the threshold of new discoveries and innovations, the future is filled with both challenges and opportunities. The journey ahead will require businesses to be resilient, adaptable, and guided by a strong moral compass.

The corporate galaxy is ever-expanding, with new technologies, markets, and business models emerging at the speed of light. As businesses navigate through this dynamic environment, they must remain vigilant, adaptable, and committed to their core values. By doing so, they can harness the opportunities of the digital age, overcome the challenges of globalization, and chart a course toward a prosperous and sustainable future.

Business is a complex and ever-changing universe, filled with challenges and opportunities. By understanding the forces of globalization and digital transformation, embracing innovation, and adhering to principles of ethical conduct and social responsibility, businesses can navigate this galaxy successfully. The journey through the corporate world of today is a voyage of discovery, requiring courage, resilience, and a forward-looking vision. As we chart our course through this vast corporate galaxy, let us do so with optimism and determination, ready to explore new horizons and seize the opportunities that lie ahead.

Data can be a rather daunting task for new businesses. Often the puzzle lies in where to begin.

2 ALIEN Challenges in the Corporate World

In the intergalactic odyssey of business, corporate captains and their crews face challenges as perplexing as an alien's crossword puzzle. These peculiar issues—data overload, communication barriers, decision-making quandaries, and the ceaseless quest for competitive edge—are like asteroids: they can catch you off guard and spin your enterprise out of orbit.

The Data Deluge: Drowning in Digital Seas

Picture this: you're the commander of a starship (i.e., a modern business), and you're navigating through an asteroid belt of data—each rock a byte, each pebble a bit. In the early days of our cosmic journey, we welcomed data like a rain in the desert. Now, we're standing with a firehose to our faces, wondering why we ever thought a downpour was a good idea.

The term "data overload" barely does justice to the tsunami of 1s and 0s that flood our systems, threatening to capsize our corporate crafts. The challenge isn't just the quantity; it's the bewildering variety. From customer insights that resemble cryptic alien signals to financial statistics that fluctuate faster than a comet's tail, businesses are often left feeling like they're playing a never-ending game of cosmic Whac-A-Mole.

Conquering this deluge demands more than a digital bucket; it requires sophisticated AI-driven pumps, designed to filter the meaningful trickles from the torrent of trivia. These systems don't just manage data; they turn it into actionable intelligence—because knowing the favorite color of your customer's pet iguana is only useful if you're selling reptile paint.

Lost in Translation: Communication Black Holes

Communication barriers in business can often feel like trying to chat at a rowdy interstellar bar—without a universal translator. Misunderstandings abound, messages get sucked into the black hole of an overfilled inbox, and the essence of the memo becomes as muddled as a martian martini.

In the cosmic expanse of the modern workplace, where remote teams operate across time zones like dispersed fleets, effective communication is both the shield and the engine for progress. Yet, we face linguistic quasars and cultural supernovas that can warp the simplest messages into incomprehensible gibberish.

To bridge these interstellar gaps, we've devised all sorts of gadgets and gizmos—from emails that zip across digital space like speedy spacecraft to collaboration platforms that act as virtual conference rooms. But let's be honest, sometimes these tools are as helpful as a chocolate teapot, and we're left nodding over video calls, hoping the Wi-Fi lag isn't making us look like we're stuck in a time loop.

Decisions, Decisions: The Paradox of Choice

Decision-making in business has its parallels to plotting a course through an asteroid field—choose wrong, and you're space dust; hesitate, and you're a sitting duck for space pirates. The contemporary corporate world provides a smorgasbord of choices, each more tantalizing than the last. Should we expand to Andromeda or focus on the Milky Way? Invest in asteroid mining or solar farming?

With data pouring in and the pressure mounting, decision fatigue can set in harder than a two-century-old fruitcake. Analysis paralysis isn't just a funny rhyme; it's a reality as teams oscillate between options like a spaceship dodging laser fire.

The key to sound decision-making isn't a bigger brain or a crystal ball (though both could come in handy). It's about leveraging the right tools and processes—think of algorithms that can predict market trends with the same certainty that the sun will rise on planet Xerox-5. Coupled with human intuition, these tools can guide us to make choices that are less like wild stabs in the dark and more like precision laser cuts.

Keeping Up with the Cosmic Joneses: Maintaining Competitiveness

In the relentless race across the corporate cosmos, maintaining competitiveness is akin to staying ahead of a supernova blast. Just when you've upgraded your star cruisers, the competition unveils their hyper-speed warp drives.

This constant one-upmanship could make a saint's halo slip. It's not just about offering the shiniest gadgets or the sleekest services; it's about anticipating what the cosmic consumer wants before they even know they want it. It's a mind-reading act that would put the best psychic to shame.

Staying competitive means tuning into the galactic grapevine, understanding the trends, and innovating faster than a shape-shifting alien. It's a delicate dance of forecasting and flexibility, where sometimes you lead, and sometimes you follow, all the while keeping your antennae tuned to the market's mercurial moods.

Charting through the Data Storm

Imagine standing amidst a meteor shower of spreadsheets and reports, each data point a potential impact. This is the daily reality for many in the business sphere. The trick isn't to dodge the shower but to weave through it, picking out patterns and pathways that lead to clarity.

In 2024, businesses harness software like Tableau for interactive and shareable dashboards, Power BI for robust analytics with seamless Microsoft integration, and Qlik Sense for user-driven data discovery. They focus on KPIs such as customer engagement metrics, operational efficiency ratios, sales conversion rates, and financial performance indicators to drive strategic decisions and gain competitive advantage.

Clear Signals in a Cosmic Static

Communication doesn't have to be as hard as explaining quantum theory to a toddler. Sometimes, it's about listening as much as speaking. In the vacuum of space, no one can hear you scream, but in the office, someone should at least hear you speak.

Creating channels that cut through the noise is essential. Modern collaboration tools are only as good as their users. It takes a culture of openness, where each voice finds a frequency that resonates, to truly conquer the void.

Modern collaboration tools widely used in 2024 include Slack for instant messaging and team communication, Microsoft Teams for comprehensive collaboration and integration with Office 365, Zoom for video conferencing and virtual meetings, Asana for project management and task coordination, and Trello for visual project tracking using kanban boards. These tools help streamline workflows, enhance team coordination, and foster a collaborative work environment regardless of geographical boundaries.

Decision-Making: Steering by Starlight

When faced with choices, a guiding star is the seasoned executive's best ally. Relying on gut feelings alone is like navigating by the seat of your spacesuit. Instead, successful leaders use a mix of data-driven insights and experience to plot their course.

They understand that the best decisions are made not in isolation but through the collective wisdom of their crew. It's about synthesizing viewpoints, much like combining different wavelengths to get the clearest picture of a distant planet.

The Innovation Race: Warp Speed Ahead

In the race for relevance, resting on your laurels is like stopping to smell the roses on an asteroid zooming toward oblivion. Competitors are relentless, their innovations as numerous as the stars. Keeping pace demands a culture where new ideas are nurtured like delicate space fauna.

The trick is to build a launchpad for innovation within your organization. Encourage experimentation and accept that not every endeavor will reach the stars. The ones that do, however, may just take you to warp speed.

Assembling Your Data Toolkit

For a fledgling enterprise taking its first steps into the data universe, the key is not to launch into the deep space of analytics without a map. Start with a clear objective: what do you want your data to tell you? Focus on customer behaviour patterns, operational efficiency, or financial health—each a beacon guiding your business decisions.

Step 1: Setting Up Your Command Center with Power BI

Begin by establishing a command center. Power BI, a user-friendly tool by Microsoft, serves as an excellent control panel, offering a dashboard that even novices can navigate. First, integrate Power BI with your sales and customer databases. Use its drag-and-drop functionality to start visualizing sales trends and customer demographics.

Step 2: Engaging with Tableau for Deeper Insights

As your confidence grows, engage with Tableau. It's like the Hubble Telescope for your data, offering deeper insights into the vast arrays of information. Create visualizations to identify which products are star performers and which may be black holes sucking in more resources than they're worth.

Step 3: Charting Unknown Territories with Qlik Sense

For more exploratory missions, turn to Qlik Sense. With its associative engine, you can make connections you didn't know existed, like finding a new planet in a familiar solar system. Qlik Sense can help you unearth hidden trends in customer data, perhaps revealing that customers who buy product X are ten times more likely to engage with product Y.

Fine-Tuning Your Communication Array

Clear communication is the plasma that powers the engines of your enterprise. As you foster a culture of transparency and collaboration, you'll find your business operations synchronizing like a well-calibrated space station.

Step 4: Establishing Channels with Slack

Start by establishing channels on Slack, where teams can discuss projects in focused streams, reducing the clutter that often fills email inboxes like space junk. With Slack, updates, questions, and ideas flow freely, keeping everyone in the loop with real-time communication.

Step 5: Expanding Horizons with Zoom

For face-to-face meetings across distances, Zoom acts as a teleportation device, bringing remote teams together with the click of a button. Use Zoom for your weekly status checks, ensuring no team member drifts off into space.

Step 6: Scheduling and Planning with Asana

Next, employ Asana for task scheduling and project planning. Asana is your mission planner, helping you track tasks from inception to completion. Set up projects, assign tasks, set deadlines, and monitor progress—all in a visually intuitive space.

Step 7: Visual Mapping with Trello

Trello offers a bird's-eye view of your projects. Much like monitoring a galaxy, Trello's boards allow you to see the status of various tasks at a glance, making sure your projects are always propelled forward, and nothing falls into a black hole.

Decision-Making: Plotting Your Course Through the Cosmos

Decisions are the steering mechanisms for your business vessel. To make them confidently, you need to gather the crew and consult the star charts—data and insights that inform your path forward.

Step 8: Consolidating Information

Consolidate your information. Bring together your data from Power BI, Tableau, and Qlik Sense. Look for consensus among the numbers; where they align, you'll find the direction you need to be heading.

Step 9: Leveraging Team Wisdom with Microsoft Teams

Bring your crew—your team—into the decision-making process with Microsoft Teams. It's a digital roundtable where each member can share insights and concerns. Collectively, you'll make decisions that are not just informed by data, but also by the human element—the intuition and experience of your team.

Sustaining Competitive Thrust

As your business grows and evolves, maintaining a competitive edge is like staying in warp drive without burning out the engines.

Step 10: Keeping a Pulse on the Market with Google Alerts

Set up Google Alerts for industry trends and competitors. It's like having a network of scouts reporting back on movements in the cosmos, ensuring you're always aware of what the competition is up to.

Step 11: Cultivating Innovation with Salesforce CRM

Embrace tools like Salesforce CRM to keep your customer relationships as strong as gravitational bonds. Use the insights gleaned from Salesforce to innovate customer service and product development, keeping you ahead of the cosmic curve.

Step 12: Staying Agile with QuickBooks for Finances

Keep your finances as nimble as a comet using QuickBooks. This financial management tool allows you to monitor cash flow in real-time, ensuring you have the resources for sudden maneuvers, whether they're market opportunities or unforeseen space debris.

KEEP IN MIND THAT AS the years pass, software may change so start with these and keep ahead with changing trends. This is as of 2024. So, if you're reading this in the future, use the guideline but use the latest software of your time. Let's continue.

STEP 13: UNDERSTAND Your Customers with Google Analytics

To really get to know the people who are buying your products or services, start using Google Analytics. It's a tool that shows you how customers behave on your website. Where do they click? What do they ignore? It's like having a telescope pointed right at your clients' habits.

Step 14: Keep Communication Crystal Clear with Dropbox

Sharing files can be messy, like trying to pass a paper note in a windstorm. Dropbox is your digital briefcase. It keeps all your documents in one place, accessible to the whole team. Say goodbye to the "Who has the latest version?" game.

Step 15: Join the Social Conversation with Hootsuite

Hootsuite is your social media command center. From here, you can send out messages, join conversations, and see what's trending across platforms like Twitter and Facebook. It's like attending a galaxy-sized party and being able to mingle in every group.

Step 16: Sharpen Your Email Game with Mailchimp

For emails that don't end up in the dreaded spam folder, Mailchimp is your go-to. It helps you design email campaigns that look good and read well on any device. It's as if you're beaming your message directly to your customers' inboxes.

Step 17: Gather Feedback with SurveyMonkey

Curious about what people think of your new product or service? Send out a survey using SurveyMonkey. It's an easy way to hear from your customers directly. Think of it as a direct line to their thoughts and opinions.

Step 18: Schedule Smart with Calendly

Organizing meetings can be like trying to synchronize watches in different time zones. Calendly does the hard work for you. Share your availability, let clients or colleagues choose a time, and voilà – the meeting's set without the back-and-forth hassle.

Step 19: Manage Customer Relationships with HubSpot

HubSpot is like your business's memory. It remembers your customers' likes, dislikes, and past conversations. Use it to tailor your approach to each customer, making them feel special and heard.

Step 20: Keep Projects on Track with Monday.com

Projects can slip away like slippery space eels if you're not careful. Monday.com helps you keep track of who's doing what and by when. It's your mission control for projects, helping everyone stay aligned and accountable.

Step 21: Stay Financially Informed with Xero

Xero keeps your financials in order. It's like a financial dashboard for your business, showing you where your money's coming from and where it's going. Use it to make smart money decisions, just like choosing the right fuel for your spaceship.

Step 22: Boost Online Sales with Shopify

If you're selling something, Shopify can help you set up your online store in no time. It's like building a marketplace on a new planet, only much easier. Design your storefront, list products, and start selling to the universe.

Step 23: Secure Your Data with Norton

In the digital realm, security is key. Norton is like your digital shield, protecting your business from viruses and cyber-attacks. It guards your data like a loyal space hound, ensuring your digital world is safe from invaders.

Step 24: Harness the Power of SEO with Moz

To make sure customers find you first, use Moz for SEO (Search Engine Optimization). It's like placing a beacon on your website that guides people through the vastness of the internet right to your digital doorstep.

TOO MUCH? LET'S SIMPLIFY it further:

Harvesting Data Wisely

Gathering data is like collecting stars. Not all of them will guide your way; choose the right ones and they will illuminate your path to success. Prioritize data that reflects customer satisfaction, sales effectiveness, and operational efficiency. Use these as your North Stars to steer by.

Simple Steps to Data Mastery:

Identify Key Performance Indicators (KPIs): These are your guiding constellations. Pick KPIs that truly reflect your business health, such as monthly sales growth, website traffic, or customer acquisition cost.

Choose a Primary Data Tool: Start with one. Power BI is integrated into many business systems, making it a universal tool for various data sources.

Train Your Team: Even the best tools need skilled operators. Invest in training so your team can navigate these tools with ease.

Review Regularly: Set a cadence for data review meetings. This keeps everyone aligned and makes data part of your operational rhythm.

Communicating Across the Cosmos

In the vacuum of space, no one can hear you scream, but in business, everyone should hear you clearly. Invest in establishing clear communication protocols from the get-go.

Simple Communication Commandments:

Use Slack for Daily Chatter: Keep day-to-day communications here. It's your intercom for quick, casual conversations.

Zoom for Face Time: Regular video check-ins maintain a personal connection, fostering trust and clarity.

Asana for Task Tracking: Assign tasks and track progress here. It's your mission log, keeping everyone accountable.

Trello for the Big Picture: Use it as your mission dashboard to visualize project progress at a glance.

Decision-Making with Confidence

Decisions are the steering thrusters of your business spaceship. Make them count with a methodical approach that combines data with human judgment.

Steps for Clear Decision-Making:

Gather Data: Use your tools to collect relevant data points.

Consult the Crew: Bring in diverse perspectives. Use Microsoft Teams to gather input and foster discussion.

Make the Call: Decisions needn't be daunting. With the right data and team input, choose a course of action.

Learn and Adapt: Every decision is a learning opportunity. Reflect on the outcomes to refine your decision-making process for the next voyage.

Maintaining Competitive Momentum

The corporate cosmos is ever-expanding, filled with businesses vying for their share of the market. Keeping your edge sharp is crucial.

Steps for Staying Competitive:

Stay Informed: Set Google Alerts for industry news and competitor updates to keep your knowledge as current as the galactic news.

Cultivate Relationships: Use Salesforce CRM to understand your customers deeply. Tailor your services to their evolving needs, just as you would adjust your sails to the cosmic winds.

Monitor Finances Closely: With QuickBooks, watch over your financial health like an eagle. Adapt spending based on your current fiscal landscape.

With these straightforward strategies and tools, even the most novice business can navigate the alien challenges of the corporate world. From wrangling the data deluge to crafting clear communication channels, making informed decisions, and staying a step ahead of the competition, these simple steps are your guide to not just surviving, but thriving among the stars.

3 The AI Expedition
Tools and Technologies

THE DAWN OF MACHINE Learning

Machine Learning (ML) is the engine that powers much of today's AI exploration. Picture it as a form of cybernetic evolution, where algorithms learn from data, adapt and make decisions, mimicking human cognition but at a scale and speed beyond our own biological capabilities.

At its core, ML uses statistical techniques to give computers the ability to 'learn' with data, without being explicitly programmed. From predictive text on smartphones to more complex recommendations for customers on retail sites, ML is omnipresent. Businesses use it to forecast sales, personalize marketing, and even guide customer service bots.

TensorFlow and PyTorch light up the skies of ML, offering frameworks for businesses to develop their own learning algorithms. These are complemented by more user-friendly platforms like Google's AutoML, which allows companies to harness machine learning even without a team of data scientists.

The Art of Natural Language Processing (NLP) is where AI comes to grips with human language, turning text and speech into something as quantifiable as numbers in a ledger. It's like a universal translator for the digital age, breaking down the barriers between human nuance and digital data.

Navigating NLP

Chatbots and Virtual Assistants Tools like IBM Watson Assistant and Google Dialogflow enable businesses to craft conversational agents that can assist customers or help employees find information quickly.

NLP algorithms can sift through customer feedback on social media, discerning the underlying sentiments and providing valuable insights into public perception.

The Mechanical Muscle of AI

Robotics, the most tangible expression of AI, combines computer intelligence with physical action. In the corporate world, robots handle everything from manufacturing tasks that are too dangerous for humans to roving warehouse shelves to fulfill orders.

Robotic Applications:

Manufacturing Automation: Companies like Fanuc and KUKA are providing robotics solutions that drive efficiency on the factory floor.

Drones for Delivery and Surveillance: Amazon's delivery drones and the surveillance drones used by security firms are expanding the boundaries of what robotics can accomplish in business logistics and security.

Predictive Analytics: Gazing into the Future

Predictive analytics uses AI to peer into the future, analyzing historical data to make predictions about upcoming trends and events. It's like having a crystal ball, but instead of vague prophecies, you get data-driven forecasts.

Predictive Tools:

Market Forecasts: Tools like SAS Predictive Analytics and IBM SPSS Modeler allow businesses to anticipate market trends, adjust stock levels, and even set dynamic pricing.

Customer Behaviour: Predictive analytics can project the future buying habits of customers, enabling businesses to tailor their strategies accordingly.

HARNESSING MACHINE Learning for Customer Insights

Businesses thrive on understanding their customers, and machine learning is the telescope that brings the distant desires of consumers into focus. With ML, companies analyse vast arrays of purchase history, online behaviour, and demographic data to uncover preferences and predict future buying behaviour.

Practical Steps with Machine Learning:

1. **Customer Segmentation**: Tools like K-Means clustering in ML platforms categorize customers into segments, enabling personalized marketing strategies.
2. **Recommendation Engines**: Using ML algorithms, businesses like Netflix and Amazon offer customers personalized recommendations, increasing satisfaction and retention.

NLP: Interpreting the Human Element

Natural Language Processing translates the complexities of human language into actionable data. Companies employ NLP to automate and enhance customer service, mine insights from social media, and even streamline internal communications.

Real-World NLP Applications:

1. **Automated Customer Support**: Chatbots powered by NLP handle routine customer queries, freeing human agents for more complex issues.
2. **Content Analysis**: Tools like Sentiment Analyser delve into the sea of online content to gauge public sentiment toward products or brands.

The Automated Workforce

Robots in the corporate world are the tireless workers, handling tasks with precision and efficiency. Beyond manufacturing, businesses deploy robots in roles from inventory management to cleaning, proving that automation can be as adaptable as it is reliable.

Robotics at Work:

1. **Warehouse Automation**: E-commerce giants like Alibaba use robotic systems to sort, pick, and pack goods, trimming down logistics costs and speeding up delivery.
2. **Service Robots**: In hospitality, robots like Hilton's Connie assist guests with information and services, adding a futuristic charm to customer service.

Predictive Analytics: Anticipating the Next Move

Predictive analytics does more than just forecast; it provides a strategic edge. By anticipating market shifts and consumer trends, businesses position themselves to meet demand before it arises, setting the pace rather than struggling to keep up.

Strategic Forecasting with Predictive Analytics:

1. **Inventory Management**: Predictive tools forecast demand, helping retailers like Walmart optimize their inventory levels, reducing waste and stockouts.
2. **Risk Assessment**: Financial institutions use predictive models to assess loan risks, identifying potential defaults before they happen and tailoring credit offerings.

Machine Learning: The Navigator of Complexity

Machine Learning has transcended the role of an autopilot for routine tasks and now serves as the navigator through the complex asteroid fields of big data.

Advancing with ML:

- **Customization at Scale**: E-commerce giants like Amazon employ ML to personalize shopping experiences, leading to increased sales and customer loyalty.
- **Optimizing Operations**: FedEx uses ML to optimize delivery routes, reducing fuel costs and improving delivery times.

Toolkit Enhancement:

- **Integration Platforms**: Platforms like MLOps offer a bridge between ML model development and operations, ensuring that businesses can scale their ML initiatives efficiently.
- **MLaaS**: Machine Learning as a Service platforms such as AWS SageMaker provide businesses with pre-built, customizable ML models, lowering the barrier to entry.

Natural Language Processing: Conversations with AI

NLP has evolved from simple text parsing to understanding context and emotions, allowing businesses to engage in meaningful conversations with customers and employees.

Conversational AI:

- **Customer Service**: Companies use chatbots, powered by NLP, to provide round-the-clock customer service. For instance, Sephora's chatbot offers beauty advice and product recommendations in real-time.
- **Voice-Activated Systems**: Google's voice search and Apple's Siri have made it possible to interact with technology hands-free, paving the way for similar applications in various industries.

Language Analytics:

- **Content Analysis**: Tools like Grammarly use NLP to improve writing quality, which is invaluable for creating clear and professional business communications.
- **Language Translation**: Services like DeepL Translator allow for near-instantaneous translation, making global communication seamless.

Robotics: Beyond the Assembly Line

Robotics has stretched its metallic limbs into realms beyond manufacturing, becoming an integral part of various service industries.

Service Robotics:

- **Healthcare**: Robots like those developed by Intuitive Surgical perform precise surgical operations, often leading to faster patient recovery times.
- **Hospitality**: Robots in hotels, such as Hilton's Connie, interact with guests, providing information and enhancing the customer experience.

Collaborative Robotics:

- **Cobots**: These are designed to work alongside humans, assisting without replacing them. Cobots are found in businesses like BMW, where they support workers with repetitive or heavy-lifting tasks.

Predictive Analytics: The Business Seer

Predictive analytics has become the seer of the business world, providing insights that drive proactive decision-making.

Operational Forecasts:

- **Inventory Management**: Retailers like Walmart use predictive analytics to manage inventory, anticipate demand spikes, and avoid overstocking or stockouts.
- **Maintenance Predictions**: Airlines utilize predictive maintenance to foresee mechanical issues, improving safety and reducing downtime.

Predictive Modeling:

- **Risk Assessment**: Financial institutions employ predictive models to assess credit risk, identifying potential defaulters before a loan is issued.
- **Market Research**: Analytical tools help businesses understand market dynamics, identifying potential opportunities or threats.

WE'VE NAVIGATED THROUGH the how's and what's of AI in business. Now, let's venture into the tangible impact of these technologies and the strategies companies adopt to harness their potential.

Embedding AI into the Customer Journey

Businesses today are embedding AI across the customer journey, from discovery to after-sales support, making interactions smoother and more personalized.

Tailored Experiences:

- **Predictive Personalization**: Netflix's recommendation engine, powered by ML, personalizes viewing suggestions, keeping subscribers engaged and reducing churn.
- **Dynamic Pricing**: Ride-sharing companies like Uber adjust prices in real-time using AI, balancing supply and demand to maximize efficiency and satisfaction.

Customer Insights:

- **Behavioural Analysis**: Platforms like Adobe Analytics use ML to track and analyse user behaviour, enabling businesses to refine their marketing strategies and website designs for optimal engagement.

Streamlining Operations with AI

AI is not just a customer-facing marvel; it streamlines operations, acting as the oil in the corporate machinery.

Efficiency and Productivity:

- **Process Automation**: Robotic Process Automation (RPA) tools like UiPath automate mundane tasks, freeing up human workers for more complex and creative work.
- **Supply Chain Optimization**: AI-powered tools by companies like Blue Yonder (formerly JDA Software) predict and manage supply chain disruptions, ensuring smoother operations.

Workforce Management:

- **HR Analytics**: LinkedIn's AI sifts through job applicant data to find the best matches for open positions, enhancing recruitment efficiency.

Fostering Innovation and New Capabilities

Innovation is the lifeblood of business, and AI acts as a catalyst, opening up new capabilities and avenues for growth.

Product Development:

- **Design and Simulation**: Autodesk's generative design software leverages AI to explore thousands of design options, finding the most efficient solutions that meet specific criteria.
- **Content Creation**: AI-powered tools like Wordsmith generate financial reports and sports recaps, allowing media companies to cover more events at a lower cost.
-

Health and Safety:

- **Workplace Safety**: Companies like Smartvid.io use AI to analyse workplace imagery for potential safety hazards, helping prevent accidents before they occur.

Challenges and Considerations in AI Adoption

With great power comes great responsibility, and AI adoption is no exception. Businesses face challenges like data privacy, ethical use of AI, and ensuring transparency.

Ethical Use and Bias Mitigation:

- **AI Ethics Policies**: Organizations are implementing AI ethics policies and guidelines to ensure fair and responsible use.
- **Bias Detection**: Tools like IBM's AI Fairness 360 detect and mitigate bias in AI algorithms, promoting fairness and equality.

Transparency and Explainability:

- **AI Explainability**: As AI decisions can have significant consequences, tools are being developed to make AI's decision-making process transparent and understandable to humans.

AI INTEGRATION: A STRATEGIC Blueprint

Successfully integrating AI into a business is akin to integrating a new reactor into a spaceship—it requires careful planning, skilled crew, and a clear understanding of the power it wields.

Developing an AI Roadmap:

- **Assess and Identify**: Evaluate your business processes to pinpoint where AI can have the most significant impact. It could be customer service, sales forecasting, or even talent management.
- **Build or Buy**: Decide whether to develop in-house AI solutions or leverage existing platforms. For many SMEs, starting with established platforms like Salesforce for customer insights or Zoho for business analytics is a practical approach.

Building a Skilled Team:

- **Upskill Existing Talent**: Invest in training programs to help current employees understand and work alongside AI. Providers like Coursera and Udacity offer courses in AI and machine learning.
- **Hire Specialists**: For more complex tasks, consider hiring AI specialists who can build custom solutions tailored to your specific needs.

Overcoming Adoption Challenges

Introducing AI into an established business structure can be as complex as performing a spacewalk. It requires not only technical know-how but also change management and cultural adaptation.

Navigating Organizational Change:

- **Leadership Buy-In**: Ensure that company leaders understand and support the AI initiative. Their endorsement is crucial for securing resources and fostering a culture receptive to AI.
- **Employee Engagement**: Engage with employees at all levels to address fears and uncertainties about AI. Clear communication about AI enhancing their roles, rather than replacing them, is vital.

Ensuring Data Governance:

- **Data Quality**: Implement rigorous data governance policies to ensure high-quality, accurate data feeds your AI systems, as poor data can lead to faulty outputs.
- **Compliance and Security**: Stay abreast of regulations like GDPR to ensure your AI solutions comply with data protection laws.
-

AI's Business Horizon: What Lies Ahead

Looking forward, the potential of AI in business is as vast as the cosmos itself. As AI technologies continue to evolve, they will open up new frontiers for innovation and competition.

Predictions for the Future:

- **Autonomous Business Processes**: In the future, we may see entire business processes autonomously managed by AI, from inventory to customer service.
- **Augmented Decision Making**: AI will augment human decision-making, offering deep insights that lead to more informed and strategic business choices.

- **Personalization at Unprecedented Scale**: Hyper-personalization will become the norm in marketing and product development, with AI crafting experiences uniquely tailored to individual preferences.

The Ethical AI Framework:

- **Developing Ethical Guidelines**: As AI becomes more influential, creating ethical guidelines will be crucial. Businesses will need to ensure that AI is used responsibly and without bias.
- **Prioritizing Human-Centric AI**: The ultimate goal of AI in business should be to augment human potential, not replace it. Companies that prioritize a human-centric approach to AI will lead the way in fostering innovation while maintaining ethical integrity.

4 Charting the Unknown: AI in Data Management

A I has emerged as an indispensable navigator, charting courses through digital seas, deciphering the complex language of data, and guiding decision-making in uncharted waters.

AI: The Master Cartographer of Data

In an era where data is the new gold, AI is the master cartographer, making sense of unstructured data with the precision of a seasoned explorer.

Data Organization and Categorization:

- **Structuring the Unstructured**: AI-powered tools like IBM Watson can organize vast repositories of unstructured data, transforming them into structured formats ready for analysis.
- **Categorization for Convenience**: AI systems categorize data automatically, tagging content and making data retrieval as simple as calling an assistant to fetch a file.

Natural Language Understanding:

- **Interpreting Human Language**: With NLP, AI translates human language data into a form that machines understand, using tools like OpenAI's GPT-3, which can generate summaries from lengthy documents, providing quick insights.

The Insight Engine: AI in Data Analysis

AI doesn't just organize data; it delves deep into it, revealing patterns and insights hidden to the human eye.

Pattern Recognition:

- **Detecting Anomalies and Trends**: AI algorithms excel at recognizing patterns, identifying anomalies in financial transactions or consumer behaviour trends that would take humans countless hours to discover.

Predictive Analysis:

- **Forecasting with AI**: Predictive analytics tools harness machine learning to forecast future trends, helping businesses prepare for what's to come. Platforms like Alteryx offer predictive modeling that businesses use to anticipate customer behaviours and market shifts.

Decision Support: AI as the Compass

In the complex decision-making process, AI acts as a compass, offering guidance rooted in data-driven objectivity.

Augmenting Human Decision-Making:

- **AI Advisory**: AI doesn't replace human decision-makers; it enhances them. Tools like Google Cloud's AI Platform provide actionable recommendations that decision-makers can use as a base for their strategies.
- **Risk Assessment**: With AI's ability to analyse vast datasets, it can assess risks far more quickly than humans, informing more secure decision-making in areas like investments and lending. Enhancing Data Accessibility and Retrieval

In the corporate data galaxy, accessibility is paramount. AI acts as the gateway, making data retrieval not just possible, but effortless.

Streamlined Data Access:

- **Search and Retrieval**: AI systems like Elasticsearch offer sophisticated search capabilities that go beyond keyword matching, understanding context and content, much like a librarian who knows every book in the library.
- **Voice-Activated Data Interaction**: Integrating voice recognition,

professionals can now query databases conversationally, using tools like Amazon Alexa for Business, to get the data they need through simple voice commands.

- The Learning Layers: AI and Machine Learning
- Beneath the surface of AI data management lies a stratified world of machine learning models, each layer learning and adapting from the one before.
-

Continuous Learning Systems:

- **Adaptive Algorithms**: Machine learning models are designed to adapt and improve over time, much like how Netflix's recommendations become more accurate the more you watch.
- **Real-Time Data Processing**: Platforms like Apache Kafka process streaming data in real time, learning and adapting at the pace of business operations.
- AI and Data Visualization: Seeing Beyond the Numbers
- Data visualization is the art of transforming numbers into narratives. AI adds depth to this art, revealing the stories hidden within datasets.
- **Automated Reporting and Dashboards:**
- **Interactive Data Storytelling**: Tools like Tableau with its AI-driven "Explain Data" feature, create narratives that explain the significance behind the data points.
- **Customized Reporting**: AI algorithms generate customized reports targeting specific KPIs, serving them to stakeholders in an easily digestible format.
- Decision-Making: The AI Consultancy
- In the boardroom of the future, AI serves as a consultant, bringing data-driven insights to the heart of business strategy.
- **Data-Driven Strategies:**
- **Strategic Planning**: AI tools analyse market data to assist in strategic planning, giving businesses a competitive edge by anticipating future trends.

- **Operational Efficiency**: AI systems evaluate operational data to recommend process optimizations, akin to a seasoned consultant advising on efficiency improvements.

Cognitive Computing: AI with Human-Like Understanding

Cognitive computing represents the next evolutionary step in AI's journey, providing businesses with systems that reason and learn much like the human brain.

Deep Learning and Neural Networks:

- **Deep Learning Applications**: These AI systems use neural networks to analyse complex patterns. For example, Google's DeepMind has been utilized in healthcare to predict patient outcomes by analysing medical records.
- **Enhancing Customer Experience**: Cognitive computing can personalize customer experiences by understanding individual preferences and behaviours, akin to a salesperson who remembers every customer's past purchases and preferences.

Real-Time Analytics: AI in the Moment

Real-time analytics powered by AI allows businesses to operate with a pulse on the present, making decisions with the most current data at their fingertips.

Streamlined Operations:

- **Instantaneous Insights**: AI-driven analytics engines, such as Apache Spark, perform real-time data analysis, enabling businesses to make informed decisions instantly.
- **Operational Agility**: With real-time analytics, businesses can dynamically adjust pricing, manage inventory levels, and respond to customer inquiries with speed and precision.

AI and the Internet of Things (IoT): A Connected Ecosystem

The fusion of AI with IoT creates a connected ecosystem where data from sensors and devices are synthesized into actionable intelligence.

Smart Infrastructure:

- **Efficient Resource Management**: AI leverages IoT data to optimize energy usage in smart buildings and predictive maintenance in manufacturing, akin to a nerve center that controls and optimizes all functions of a facility.
- **Connected Devices**: In retail, smart shelves equipped with IoT sensors monitor stock levels and customer interactions, sending data back to an AI system that manages inventory and provides insights on shopping behaviours.

The Future of Data Security: AI as the Guardian

As businesses become more data-centric, the role of AI in ensuring data security becomes critical.

Proactive Threat Detection:

- **Advanced Security Protocols**: AI-driven security platforms, such as Darktrace, use machine learning to detect and respond to cyber threats in real-time, often before human operators are aware of an issue.
- **Fraud Prevention**: AI systems in financial institutions analyse transaction patterns to identify and prevent fraudulent activities, acting as a vigilant watchdog over customer accounts.

Preparing for an AI-Driven Data Future

Embracing the AI Data Revolution:

- **Cultural Shift**: Businesses must foster a culture that embraces AI, with continuous learning and adaptation at its core.
- **Investment in AI Infrastructure**: Investing in the right AI

infrastructure, including hardware and software, is crucial for businesses to leverage the full potential of AI in data management.

- **Ethical Data Practices**: Establishing a framework for ethical AI use ensures that as businesses grow more intelligent with data, they also maintain integrity and trust.

The AI-Infused Workforce: Collaboration and Empowerment

The modern workplace is witnessing a transformation, as AI becomes a collaborator, augmenting human capabilities and empowering a more efficient workforce.

Human-AI Collaboration:

- **Cobotics**: Robots that work alongside humans, or 'cobots', are becoming commonplace in industries from automotive to electronics, enhancing productivity and safety.
- **AI in Talent Management**: AI-driven HR systems, like LinkedIn's Talent Solutions, assist in identifying and recruiting top talent, optimizing the match between job requirements and applicant attributes.

Enhancing Skills and Productivity:

- **AI-Enabled Training Platforms**: Services like Pluralsight use AI to personalize learning paths for employees, aligning skills development with business needs.
- **Productivity Tools**: AI-powered productivity tools, such as Microsoft's MyAnalytics, provide employees with insights into their work patterns, promoting healthier work habits and greater productivity.

AI for Business Intelligence: The Decision-Maker's Telescope

AI extends its reach into the realm of business intelligence, turning data into strategic foresight.

Informed Decision-Making:

- **Advanced BI Tools**: Tools like Qlik Sense harness AI to turn complex data analyses into intuitive reports, dashboards, and visualizations.
- **Competitive Intelligence**: AI systems crawl through vast expanses of public and private data to provide businesses with intelligence on competitors' activities, akin to a telescope trained on distant galaxies.

Ethical AI Deployment: Navigating the Moral Compass

As businesses increasingly rely on AI, they must navigate the ethical considerations of its deployment, ensuring that AI remains a force for good.

Establishing Ethical Guidelines:

- **Frameworks for Ethical AI**: Initiatives like the AI Fairness 360 toolkit by IBM help businesses audit their AI models for bias and fairness.
- **Transparency in AI Systems**: Companies are working towards creating transparent AI systems that make decisions understandable and explainable for humans, crucial for maintaining trust and accountability.

AI Governance: Steering the Ship Responsibly

AI governance is the steering mechanism, ensuring that the business ship navigates responsibly in the AI-driven waters.

Creating Governance Structures:

- **AI Oversight Committees**: These bodies set the course for responsible AI deployment and monitor its adherence to ethical standards.
- **Regulatory Compliance**: Keeping abreast of AI regulations, businesses ensure their AI strategies comply with laws and guidelines, preventing breaches and ensuring customer trust.

AI in Decision-Making: Beyond Data Management

The journey of AI extends beyond managing data; it transforms into an integral decision-maker within organizations, providing insights that drive pivotal business decisions.

Automated Decision Engines:

- **Automated Decision-Making**: Systems like ZestFinance use AI to assist with loan approvals, automating decisions based on a multitude of data points that would be inscrutable to a human analyst.
- **Strategic Game Changers**: AI-driven platforms such as Palantir inform strategic decisions, from optimizing logistics to preemptive equipment maintenance in heavy industries.

Bridging Gaps with AI: Integration Across Departments

AI's ability to integrate and analyse data across departments bridges organizational gaps, creating a cohesive, interconnected business environment.

Cross-Departmental Synergy:

- **Unified Data Platforms**: Salesforce's Einstein Analytics is an example of an AI platform that provides a 360-degree view of the customer, enhancing collaboration between sales, marketing, and customer service teams.
- **Workflow Automation**: AI systems streamline workflows across departments, ensuring that operations like procurement, HR, and finance are synchronized, reducing bottlenecks and increasing productivity.

Advanced Analytics: Predicting and Shaping the Future

Advanced analytics powered by AI doesn't just predict the future; it helps shape it by providing businesses with the foresight to craft their destinies.

Prescriptive Analytics:

- **Crafting Future Strategies**: Tools like IBM's Watson Analytics not only predict outcomes but also prescribe actions, recommending strategies to achieve desired business goals.
- **Dynamic Market Adaptation**: AI's ability to analyse and predict market conditions allows businesses to adapt dynamically, adjusting marketing strategies and product development in response to emerging trends.

AI as a Catalyst for Innovation

AI acts as a catalyst for innovation, pushing businesses to explore new products, services, and markets.

Innovation Incubator:

- **Product Innovation**: AI tools analyse consumer data to suggest new product features or entirely new products, driving innovation based on actual consumer needs and market gaps.
- **Exploring New Markets**: AI insights can identify untapped markets, guiding businesses to expand their reach and explore new opportunities for growth.

The Human-AI Partnership

The most successful businesses will be those that understand AI as a partner to human creativity and intuition, not a replacement.

Collaborative Creativity:

- **Enhancing Human Creativity**: AI can assist designers and creators by providing them with a starting point for their creations, as seen with Autodesk's generative design software.
- **Human-AI Teams**: Companies like Google are developing AI that works alongside humans, enhancing human decision-making rather than supplanting it.

We are now at the precipice of a new era in which AI not only supports but actively enhances the fundamental processes of business operation. As we embrace this partnership with AI, we stand ready to reshape the world of project management and resource allocation, ensuring a more efficient, responsive, and intelligent business environment.

5 Overcoming Communication Black Holes

A‍I technologies are spearheading a revolution in corporate communication, tearing down the black holes that once devoured clear and effective interaction. This chapter will be an easy read, aimed at elucidating the complex world of AI communication tools in a way that feels as breezy as a conversation with a good friend.

AI and the Art of Conversation: The Rise of Chatbots

AI chatbots has transformed the landscape of customer service. They're the tireless attendants that never sleep, always ready to assist.

Friendly Front-Desk Bots:

- **24/7 Customer Service**: Chatbots like those deployed by Bank of America's Erica can handle a range of queries, from balance inquiries to transaction histories, any time of day.
- **Handling High Volume**: During sales or product launches, AI chatbots can manage the influx of questions, ensuring every customer feels heard.

Chatbots as Brand Ambassadors:

- **Consistent Brand Voice**: With every interaction, chatbots can embody the voice and values of the brand, providing a consistent experience.
- **Feedback and Learning**: These AI systems learn from each interaction, continually improving their ability to communicate effectively and empathetically.

CRM: The AI-Enhanced Backbone of Customer Relationships

Customer Relationship Management (CRM) systems are the backbone of any business's interactions with customers. When fueled by AI, they become powerful engines driving personalized experiences.

Intuitive Customer Insights:

- **Predictive Customer Service**: AI-driven CRMs, such as Salesforce Einstein, anticipate customer needs and suggest solutions, often before the customer recognizes the need themselves.
- **Personalization at Scale**: With AI, CRMs can tailor communication to the individual preferences and history of each customer, as if each has their own personal account manager.

Breaking Language Barriers: Automated Translations

In a global marketplace, language barriers can be formidable. AI-powered translation tools serve as bridges, enabling clear and accurate cross-cultural communication.

Real-Time Language Translation:

- **Instant Understanding**: Tools like Google Translate now offer real-time translation services, enabling instant understanding in multilingual meetings or negotiations.
- **Cultural Nuance Recognition**: Advances in NLP allow for the recognition of cultural nuances, idioms, and colloquialisms, leading to translations that are not just accurate but also culturally sensitive.

AI in Email Communication: Crafting Clarity

Email remains a cornerstone of business communication. AI is revolutionizing this domain, ensuring messages are clear, concise, and free of ambiguity.

Smart Compose and Reply:

- **Efficient Email Drafting**: Gmail's Smart Compose feature suggests complete sentences as you type, streamlining email creation.

- **Intelligent Response Suggestions**: AI also offers quick replies based on email content, saving time and maintaining the flow of communication.

The Integration of AI in Telecommunications

Telecommunications is no longer just about making calls. AI integrates with telecommunication systems to enhance connectivity and data exchange.

Advanced Call Routing:

- **Smart Call Distribution**: AI algorithms analyse caller data and intent, routing calls to the most suitable department or representative.
- **Voice Analysis for Quality Control**: AI tools monitor call quality and customer satisfaction by analyzing voice patterns and inflections.

VIRTUAL ASSISTANTS: Beyond Simple Chatbots

Virtual assistants, the evolved cousins of chatbots, handle complex tasks with a personal touch, from managing calendars to setting reminders.

Proactive Assistance:

- **Personalized Scheduling**: AI like x.ai can coordinate with multiple parties to find the best meeting times, juggling calendars with ease.
- **Smart Task Management**: Virtual assistants can prioritize tasks based on urgency and personal work habits, ensuring nothing falls through the cracks.

AI-Driven CRM: Nurturing Customer Relationships

CRM systems augmented with AI are not just repositories of customer data; they're active participants in nurturing customer relationships.

Deep Learning for Deep Relationships:

- **Behavioural Predictions**: By analysing past interactions, AI can predict future customer behaviour, allowing for proactive engagement.
- **Sentiment Tracking**: AI in CRM systems gauges customer sentiment, signalling when to celebrate customer loyalty or intervene to prevent churn.

Automated Translations: The Lingua Franca of Business

As businesses expand globally, automated translation tools become essential in maintaining clear and effective communication across language divides.

Cultural Adaptation:

- **Localized Marketing**: AI-powered translations enable businesses to tailor their marketing materials to local languages and customs, resonating with a diverse customer base.
- **Document Translation**: Instantaneous and accurate document translations by AI make international collaboration seamless.

AI-Enhanced Internal Communication

Within an organization, AI facilitates a clear and open communication culture, bridging departments and hierarchies.

Streamlined Information Sharing:

- **Knowledge Bases**: AI systems create and manage extensive knowledge bases, making information accessible to all employees, promoting transparency and collaboration.
- **Internal Networking**: AI-driven platforms suggest internal experts for specific projects or problems, fostering a network of in-house collaboration.

The Future of AI in External Communication

Looking outward, AI is set to revolutionize how businesses interact with the world.

Global PR and Social Media:

- **AI-Curated Content**: AI tools curate content for social media, targeting posts to reach the right audience at the right time.
- **Automated PR Responses**: AI systems can provide initial responses to press inquiries, ensuring timely and consistent communication.

———————

THE VIRTUAL ASSISTANTS of today are far from the robotic voices of the past; they are the tireless personal secretaries, the behind-the-scenes orchestrators of efficiency. Picture a virtual assistant that not only schedules your meetings with the acumen of a seasoned executive assistant but also nudges you to send a birthday greeting to a client, enhancing relationships with a human touch.

On the customer relationship front, AI-driven CRM systems have become the stewards of client connections. They hold the thread of each customer's story, analyzing and predicting needs with an intimacy that belies their silicon origins. These systems, ever-learning and adapting, are the watchful guardians of customer satisfaction, armed with the foresight to anticipate and react to the subtle shifts in customer sentiment.

The story of AI in business communication transcends the boundaries of language. Automated translation tools are the diligent diplomats, bridging conversations and connecting commerce across the global tapestry. They work in silent efficiency, allowing marketing messages to resonate with local color and enabling documents to flow freely between collaborators, unimpeded by the barrier of language.

Within the vast ecosystem of a company, AI has become the great communicator, the central hub of a wheel that connects spokes running through every department and team. It is the creator and custodian of knowledge bases, the silent archivist that ensures wisdom is shared and silos are dismantled. AI platforms, acting on insights gleaned from patterns of communication, suggest connections, pairing questions to experts, needs to providers, and fostering an environment of collective intelligence.

As businesses reach out to the world, AI stands at the helm of global PR and social media, a master of ceremonies for the digital age. It curates content with the precision of a seasoned editor, ensuring that messages not only reach their intended audiences but sing with relevance and timeliness. In the rapid-response world of PR, AI systems stand ready to offer the first handshake, delivering responses that maintain the harmony of a company's voice.

6 AI and the Art of Navigation

Navigating the modern corporate seas requires more than just a good sense of direction; it demands a depth of understanding that can anticipate the currents and winds before they are even felt. Here, AI emerges as the seasoned navigator, a tool no longer auxiliary but central to maintaining the course of the corporate ship amidst the ever-changing tides of the business landscape.

AI: The Steersman of Project Management

In the realm of project management, AI has become the steersman, with hands firm on the wheel, guiding projects from inception to completion.

Project Planning and Forecasting: With AI, project managers can predict outcomes with greater accuracy. Machine learning algorithms, trained on historical data, can forecast project timelines and identify potential delays before they occur. AI, therefore, serves as a looking glass into the future of a project's path.

Risk Management: Identifying risks is one of the key responsibilities of a project manager. AI systems, adept at pattern recognition, can sense the subtle signals that indicate potential project risks, allowing teams to address issues proactively rather than reactively.

Resource Scheduling: AI excels at optimizing schedules and resources. It considers the complexity of tasks, individual team member's strengths and weaknesses, and the intricacies of the project's requirements to formulate the most effective deployment of human and material resources.

AI in Workflow Optimization: The Silent Conductor

Workflow optimization is where AI truly conducts its symphony, orchestrating various elements of the business process to play in harmony.

Process Automation: Robotic Process Automation (RPA) employs AI to perform repetitive tasks, learning and improving as it goes. It's the workhorse that never tires, handling everything from data entry to complex analytical tasks, freeing human counterparts to focus on strategic planning and creative problem-solving.

Adaptive Workflows: AI systems are not just rigid automatons; they're like the adaptable navigators of old, capable of adjusting their course based on the stars and the seas. In the corporate context, this means machine learning algorithms that dynamically adjust workflows, anticipating bottlenecks, and redistributing tasks to maintain smooth operational sailing.

Seamless Integration: AI acts as the glue that binds disparate systems and software, allowing for seamless data flow between them. It ensures that information is where it needs to be, akin to a skilled crew member who anticipates the needs of their shipmates, passing the right tool at the right time without being asked.

AI and Resource Allocation: The Astute Quartermaster

Resource allocation, when done correctly, ensures that every part of the corporate vessel is adequately equipped for the journey ahead. AI takes on the role of the quartermaster, meticulously managing resources to prevent both excess and scarcity.

Predictive Allocation: With its ability to analyse vast quantities of data, AI can predict where resources will be needed most, often before the need arises. It assesses the winds and the tides—the market trends and internal company metrics—to ensure that resources are allocated efficiently.

Cost Optimization: AI looks at resource allocation through the lens of cost-benefit analysis, often revealing surprising areas where savings can be made without sacrificing performance. It finds the most economical routes, avoiding the storms of wasteful expenditure.

———

CASE STUDIES: AI'S Success at the Helm

Walmart's AI-Driven Supply Chain Optimization

Walmart employs AI and machine learning (ML) predictions to optimize its supply chain, placing inventory strategically across its network to meet demand efficiently. This advanced use of technology enables Walmart to handle daily operations, including peak customer traffic periods like Black Friday, without noticeable disruption. AI also prepares the company for unforeseen events, such as natural disasters, by simulating scenarios and offering actionable plans. This capability was particularly useful during Hurricane Ian, as AI allowed Walmart to reroute shipments to meet increased demand following the weather event. This approach underscores the essential role of AI in retail supply chain operations, with three-quarters of retailers acknowledging its importance according to an IDC report.

Zara's Just-In-telligent Supply Chain Management

Zara takes a comprehensive and holistic approach to AI, integrating it across all business operations, including supply chain and inventory management. Unlike its competitors, Zara minimizes outsourcing, enabling greater control and data collection at every business stage. The company utilizes RFID tagging, real-time analytics, and machine learning for inventory optimization and to rapidly respond to market trends. This approach has enabled Zara to achieve a turnaround time for new designs of as little as one week, significantly below the industry average, enhancing customer satisfaction and loyalty. Challenges such as data management and the integration of AI into existing systems are met with skilled human resources to maintain and optimize these advanced systems. The Journey of a Tech Titan: A tech titan used AI to streamline its project management across global teams. The AI provided forecasts and identified potential delays, adjusting timelines and resources on the fly. This AI navigator ensured that not a single project veered off course, even in the choppiest of international waters.

AI as the Engine of Workflow Innovation

AI does not merely maintain the status quo; it drives innovation, pushing workflows into new realms of efficiency and creativity.

Creative Workflow Solutions: In the advertising world, AI has begun managing workflows for creative projects, analyzing past campaign data to guide the creative process towards likely successful outcomes. It's as if the AI is the creative director's muse, whispering insights gleaned from a thousand campaigns into the ear of the creative team.

Intelligent Automation: In finance, RPA bots have taken over routine tasks like data reconciliation and report generation. But beyond this, AI has begun to provide insights into cash flow patterns, suggesting changes to payment terms or credit lines that a human might not consider.

Navigating Human Resources with AI

The most precious resource aboard any ship is its crew. AI plays a crucial role in managing this human capital, ensuring that the right person is in the right role and that morale remains high.

Talent Acquisition and Retention: AI-driven HR systems are capable of scanning through thousands of resumes to find the perfect fit for a position, and once hired, they can help manage employee satisfaction and career development, ensuring that the company not only finds but also retains the brightest stars.

AI for Employee Development: Through personalized training programs and career pathing powered by AI, employees are given the tools to navigate their own career journeys within the company, fostering a sense of growth and opportunity.

AI AND STRATEGIC DECISION-Making: The Compass for Leaders

AI has evolved to become the compass by which business leaders set their strategic directions, leveraging vast oceans of data to inform decisions that once relied solely on human intuition.

Data-Driven Leadership: At the forefront of this evolution, CEOs and executives now turn to AI for insights on market trends, competitive analysis, and internal performance metrics. Like ancient mariners relying on the stars, today's leaders rely on AI to chart their company's course through competitive waters.

Enhancing Boardroom Discussions: AI doesn't replace the boardroom; it enhances it. By providing comprehensive reports and predictive scenarios, AI arms decision-makers with the information needed to debate, deliberate, and decide on the future of their enterprises.

The AI Advisor in Marketing and Sales

Marketing and sales departments have found a sage advisor in AI, which offers not only insights into customer behaviour but also predictions about future market trends.

Personalization at Scale: Imagine a world where every marketing message or product recommendation is tailored to the individual preferences of each customer. AI makes this a reality, analyzing customer data to personalize interactions at a scale unimaginable to human marketers.

Sales Forecasting: Sales teams now look to AI to forecast future sales with a degree of accuracy that allows for precise planning and resource allocation. These AI-driven forecasts become the backbone of sales strategies, guiding teams on where to focus their efforts for maximum return.

Workflow and Operations: AI as the Master Planner

Within the daily operations of a business, AI serves as the master planner, optimizing workflows to ensure the smooth operation of the corporate machinery.

Supply Chain Optimization: In supply chains, AI predicts disruptions and automates reactions, such as rerouting shipments or adjusting inventory levels before a potential issue becomes a crisis. It's the equivalent of a seasoned sailor predicting storms on the horizon and adjusting the sails before the wind changes.

Resource Allocation: AI's analytical capabilities shine in resource allocation, where it assesses project needs, employee capabilities, and available assets to assign resources most effectively. Like a skilled quartermaster, AI ensures that every part of the company is equipped for its specific challenges.

———

ONWARD WE SAIL, WITH AI as our steadfast companion, discovering how it not only navigates but also redraws the maps of corporate strategy and operations.

AI in Project Management: A New Epoch

The landscape of project management has been forever altered by AI's capacity to envision and execute with precision. AI systems serve as the architects of time and task management, providing a scaffold upon which human ingenuity can build more freely.

Dynamic Project Adaptation: AI in project management is like having a skilled helmsman who can anticipate and navigate around stormy weather long before it appears on the horizon. Tools like Asana's "Workload" feature consider team capacity, helping to balance work distribution and avoid burnout.

The Predictive Powerhouse: Leveraging historical data, AI can make educated guesses about project timelines and outcomes. This predictive prowess means potential issues can be addressed long before they manifest, allowing for a smoother journey towards project milestones.

Workflow Optimization: The AI Conductor

AI is not only a participant in workflow optimization; it is the conductor, orchestrating each move to create a seamless ballet of business processes.

Intelligent Automation: AI-driven automation tools are not merely reactive but proactive, learning from ongoing processes and adapting in real-time. For example, AI in services like Zapier can suggest workflow enhancements based on user actions and repeated patterns.

Connecting Islands of Data: In the digital sea, data often exists in isolated islands. AI is the bridge-builder, creating data conduits that allow for unprecedented levels of collaboration and efficiency. An AI system integrating data across platforms is akin to constructing a grand causeway where previously there were only disjointed paths.

Resource Allocation: The AI Economist

In resource allocation, AI plays the economist, analyzing market forces, internal capabilities, and a plethora of variables to ensure resources are invested wisely.

Resource Forecasting: Just as a meteorologist forecasts weather, AI forecasts the resource needs of the business. It can predict when additional human resources are needed or when it's time to scale back, maintaining an equilibrium between supply and demand.

Optimizing for Cost and Efficiency: AI's role in resource allocation is not only about maintaining balance but also about optimizing for cost and efficiency. By continuously analyzing data, AI systems like IBM's Watson can suggest where to cut costs without sacrificing quality or output, ensuring the corporate ship sails efficiently and economically.

WE STAND AT THE HELM with AI as our compass, looking toward the future it's charting—a future that promises even greater integration of intelligence across every facet of business operations.

The AI-Infused Future of Project Management

Project management's future, infused with AI, hints at a landscape where foresight and adaptability are built into the very framework of execution. AI will not only manage timelines and resources but also contribute creatively, offering solutions to complex problems and innovating project approaches.

Project Innovation: AI could suggest alternative project methodologies based on the unique constraints and goals of each venture, much like a wise advisor who has seen countless projects to successful completion.

Enhanced Team Dynamics: By understanding team strengths and stress points, AI could manage not just the flow of tasks but also the ebb of team morale, keeping the human element at the forefront of project success.

Workflow Optimization: AI as the Heartbeat of Business

AI's role in workflow optimization will continue to expand, becoming the heartbeat that ensures the health and vitality of business processes.

Predictive Workflow Design: Imagine AI that can design workflows based on predicted market changes, customer demands, or even global trends, ensuring businesses are always a step ahead.

Adaptive Learning Systems: Workflow systems will learn and adapt not yearly or monthly, but moment-to-moment, constantly fine-tuning the orchestration of tasks and information.

Resource Allocation: The Strategic Commander

In resource allocation, AI will take on the role of a strategic commander, deploying assets where they will be most effective, often before the need is fully articulated.

Global Resource Networks: AI will manage resources on a global scale, navigating the complexities of international markets, supply chains, and workforce distribution with an understanding that is both broad and deep.

Sustainable Resource Use: AI will be pivotal in driving businesses towards sustainability, allocating resources in ways that minimize environmental impact while maximizing economic return.

7 Innovating New World

Let's talk about pioneers—not the ones who traversed continents, but those who are redrawing the boundaries of what businesses can achieve with AI. Picture a world where every new venture starts with the question, "How can AI not just improve but redefine our product or service?"

The Personal Shopper AI

Imagine walking into a store where the AI knows your taste better than you do. A retail company did just that—they created a virtual stylist. Using AI to analyse past purchases, browsing habits, and even current trends, the system suggests items that fit your style and budget. It's not pushy; it's intuitive, a digital confidante that knows the difference between what you'll admire and what you'll wear.

The Healthcare Revolution

There's a healthcare provider that has an AI which predicts patient health risks. Picture a system that looks at your medical history, lifestyle, and even your genetic markers. It's not playing doctor; it's supporting them, providing a second opinion that's rooted in data, not gut feeling. This AI doesn't just look at your chart; it reads between the lines, finding the patterns that could signify something more.

The Green Factory

Consider a manufacturing plant where AI optimizes energy use. Sensors throughout the facility collect data on machine use, energy spikes, and idle times. The AI is like an ever-vigilant eco-warrior, suggesting machine downtimes to coincide with peak solar output or dialing back HVAC when the factory floor is empty. It's manufacturing with a conscience, guided by intelligence that's as concerned with the bottom line as it is with the planet.

AI and the Artisan

Now, think about a company that pairs AI with artisans to design unique products. The AI suggests designs based on current trends and material availability, but it's the human touch that brings them to life. It's a symbiotic relationship; the AI brings the data, and the artisans bring the soul.

AI is everywhere, like glitter at a craft fair. But let's talk about those who are not just sprinkling the glitter but shaping it into something dazzling. These are the companies that saw AI not as a shiny new toy but as Play-Doh to mold innovations that we hadn't even dreamed of.

The Titans of Retail: A Personalized Shopping Universe

Let's start with the retail behemoths, shall we? You know who I'm talking about—the kind of stores you can get lost in for hours. They've been using AI to make sure you find exactly what you're looking for, sometimes before you even know you're looking for it.

Take, for instance, the case of Retail Rhapsody. They took AI and turned it into a personal shopping assistant, not the kind that follows you around the store, but the digital kind that remembers that you looked at a pair of shoes last week and sends you a coupon for them, just as you were thinking, "I should buy those."

The Wizards of Streaming: Custom Playlists in the Making

And how about the streaming services, eh? They've been crafting playlists and recommending shows with an eerie precision that makes you think, "Is this AI reading my mind?"

StreamWorld, oh, they're a crafty bunch. Their AI algorithms are like DJs at the world's biggest party, knowing just what to play next to keep you on the dance floor—that is, glued to your screen.

Banking on AI: The Financial Oracles

The financial world has its own AI champions, like Fiscal Future, who turned AI into an oracle for investments. Their AI doesn't just crunch numbers; it sees patterns in the economy that are invisible to mere mortals, offering investment advice that has turned many a small investor into a modern-day Croesus.

Health Pioneers: Diagnostics with a Digital Twist

Healthcare, too, has its AI revolutionaries. Companies like MediMinds are using AI for diagnostics that can read an MRI faster than you can say "magnetic resonance imaging" and with enough accuracy to make you wonder if AI has a medical degree.

Food Industry Innovators: Taste-Making and Baking

Now, let's not forget the food industry. There's GastroGenius, who's using AI to craft recipes that might seem bizarre at first—like chocolate-flavored fish—but end up being an unexpected hit on the taste buds.

Automotive Adventurers: Self-Driving and Thriving

And cars! Self-driving vehicles were once the stuff of science fiction, but companies like AutoAdvance are making them a reality. Their AI systems aren't just about taking you from point A to B; they're about doing it in style and with a level of safety that has you feeling like you're in a sci-fi movie.

Business Model Disruptors: Subscription Over Ownership

Lastly, let's talk about those changing the very idea of ownership. AccessOverAssets has turned everything into a subscription service. Why own when AI can predict exactly when you'll need something, for how long, and then ensure it's at your doorstep? That's not business; that's wizardry!

Now, if you're thinking that AI innovation is all about big players and deep pockets, think again. The startup scene is buzzing with David-versus-Goliath tales, thanks to the slingshot of AI.

Boutique E-tailers: Hyper-Personalized Online Shopping

There's ChicBoutique, a small online retailer that could give the retail giants a run for their money. Their AI digs deep into customer data to craft a personalized shopping experience. Picture walking into a store where everything on the shelf is precisely what you love. That's their website, thanks to AI.

EdTech Visionaries: Customized Learning Paths

Or consider LearnSphere, an EdTech startup. They're using AI to personalize learning paths so intricately that each student feels like they have their own private tutor, guiding them through their educational journey.

GreenTech Crusaders: AI for a Sustainable Future

Then we have the GreenTech crusaders like EcoAI. They're meshing AI with environmental science to optimize everything from energy consumption in buildings to reducing waste in manufacturing processes. It's like Mother Nature got herself an AI-powered shield.

Fintech Innovators: Democratizing Finance

Let's not forget the fintech innovators. WealthWise is using AI to break down complex financial advice into nuggets of wisdom that even a kid with a piggy bank could understand. They're democratizing finance, making the market accessible to the average Joe and Jane.

Social Media Mavens: Curating Content with Precision

And social media? That's a whole other realm. SocialSavvy, a rising star in the social media galaxy, uses AI to curate content so relevant that users feel like it's reading their minds. They're not just liking posts; they're loving them, thanks to AI's uncanny knack for content curation.

Hospitality Heroes: AI-Powered Customer Delight

In hospitality, there's HostHaven, with AI that tailors the guest experience to such a degree that every room feels like home. The AI anticipates needs you didn't know you had. Extra pillows? A guide to the city's hidden gems? It's already there, thanks to the AI concierge.

Logistics Leaders: Predictive Shipping and Handling

And in the world of logistics, FastForward is using AI to predict shipping delays before they happen. They're like the meteorologists of logistics, ensuring your package avoids the storms and arrives on time.

SO, WE'VE SEEN AI STIR up revolutions in every industry it touches, but what about the industries that didn't even exist until AI waved its magic wand?

AI in Agriculture: From Seedling to Superfood

Let's mosey on over to the agricultural fields. We've got AgriTech Innovations, a company that's pioneering 'precision farming.' Their AI algorithms analyse soil data, weather patterns, and even satellite images to tell farmers exactly when to plant, what to plant, and where. The result? Crops that are healthier, yields that are higher, and food that's more nutritious. It's like AI has a green thumb.

The Architects of Augmented Reality

Next, let's slip on the VR goggles and glance at the wizards behind Virtual Ventures. They're using AI to create augmented reality experiences that are so immersive, you might forget which reality you belong to. Whether it's for gaming, education, or virtual tourism, they're crafting worlds that are limited only by imagination.

The Pioneers of Personal Health

Let's also chat about those who are bringing the doctor's office into the living room. Health-at-Home provides personalized medical analysis through AI, turning your smart devices into health monitors. With a few taps and swipes, AI is keeping tabs on your health, offering advice and alerts. It's like having a tiny doctor in your pocket.

The Game Changers of Public Safety

And in public safety, there's SafeStreet Solutions. They've developed AI systems that assist law enforcement by analyzing public data, recognizing patterns, and identifying areas where resources are needed most. It's as though the AI is the city's guardian angel, watching over the streets.

AI in Space: The Final Frontier

Now, let's launch into space with Stellar Exploration Inc.. These folks are using AI to interpret massive amounts of data from telescopes and space probes, identifying potential new planets and even assisting in the search for extraterrestrial life. With AI, they're not just reaching for the stars; they're grabbing hold of them.

The Fashion Forward: AI-Designed Couture

Finally, let's strut down the runway with CoutureAI. They're bringing high fashion to the masses by using AI to design clothing based on current trends, body types, and customer preferences. They're not just designing clothes; they're weaving the fabric of future fashion.

8 Crewmates and AI: Collaboration not Competition

———

Here, the crew is an eclectic mix of humans and AI. The humans, with their innate creativity and emotional intelligence, and the AI, with its vast analytical capabilities and relentless efficiency, are not at odds but in concert. They are collaborators, each bringing their unique strengths to the deck.

The Creative Compass Meets the Analytical Anchor

The beauty of this partnership lies in the balance. Human creativity acts as the compass, guiding the direction with innovation and intuition. AI provides the anchor, grounding decisions in data and logic.

The Design Duo: Consider the world of design. AI now offers tools that can generate hundreds of logo designs in minutes, but it's the human designer who adds the nuance, understanding the brand's story and the emotional impact of each curve and color.

The Writer and the Wordsmith: In writing, AI offers assistance with grammar and style, but it's the human touch that weaves the narrative, crafts the compelling argument, or delivers the punchline.

Collaboration in Complex Problem-Solving

When tackling complex problems, the human-AI team is a formidable one.

The Doctor and the Data: Look at healthcare, where AI helps diagnose diseases by analyzing medical images with superhuman speed and precision. Yet, it's the doctor who looks the patient in the eye and offers a treatment plan with compassion and understanding.

The Trader and the Trend Analyst: In finance, AI algorithms can detect market trends and suggest trades, but it's the financial expert who understands the subtleties of the market and the needs of their clients, making the final call.

AI in Supportive Roles: Amplifying Human Potential

AI excels in supportive roles that amplify human potential, freeing us from mundane tasks to pursue more creative and strategic endeavors.

The Assistant to the Strategist: Administrative AI tools take care of scheduling and email management, but it's the strategist who uses the time saved to plan the next big move.

The Analyst and the Decision Maker: AI can crunch numbers and analyse data at an unparalleled pace, but it's the human manager who interprets these analyses within the broader context of business goals and team morale.

THE EDUCATORS AND THE Algorithm

Education has always been a human-centric field, and it remains so, but AI is now the teacher's aide that never tires.

Tailored Learning Experiences: AI systems analyse how students learn, adapting educational content to suit individual paces and learning styles. But it's the teacher who understands the nuances of each student's struggles and triumphs, shaping lessons with empathy and insight.

Administrative Efficiency: AI handles the grading and administration, but educators infuse the learning process with mentorship and guidance, offering a personal touch that no algorithm can replicate.

The Engineers and the Machine Minds

In engineering, the convergence of human and AI is like a duet between imagination and precision.

Design Beyond Limits: AI provides simulations and calculations that push the limits of traditional engineering, but it's the human engineer who dreams up the innovations that AI tests against the laws of physics.

Predictive Maintenance: AI predicts when machines will need maintenance, but it's the engineer who understands the wear and tear that machinery undergoes, translating AI's data into practical action.

The Filmmakers and the Editing Bots

The movie industry is another realm where this partnership plays out in technicolor.

Scriptwriting Assistants: AI tools suggest plot twists and dialogue based on audience preferences and genre trends, but it's the screenwriter who infuses the story with emotional depth and originality.

Post-Production Perfection: AI can edit hours of footage down to the best takes, but it's the director's creative vision that brings the story to life, deciding not just which shots to keep but why they matter.

The Scientists and the Data Decoders

In research and development, scientists and AI are co-explorers, uncovering truths hidden in data.

Complex Analysis: AI processes vast datasets faster than any human could, but it's the scientist who asks the questions that lead to discovery, interpreting AI's findings through the lens of human curiosity and knowledge.

Innovative Solutions: AI accelerates the pace of innovation, sifting through millions of compounds to find potential new drugs, but it's the researcher who understands the implications of these discoveries for human health and well-being.

THE FUTURE OF WORK: A Symbiotic Workplace

Imagine a workplace where AI doesn't replace jobs but enriches them.

Elevating Expertise: AI systems handle the drudgery of data, allowing professionals to ascend to new heights of strategic thinking and innovation. Accountants, lawyers, and doctors all find AI to be less of a rival and more of a partner that provides the informational backbone for their expertise.

Collaborative Creative Processes: In creative industries, AI tools serve as muses and assistants, offering artists, writers, and designers a springboard for their creativity—generating ideas that humans refine, reshape, and bring to fruition.

AI and the Enhancement of Daily Life

The collaboration between humans and AI isn't confined to office walls; it permeates the fabric of daily life.

Assistive Technologies for Well-being: In homes, AI personal assistants are evolving to provide not just reminders and entertainment but also to support mental and physical health, acting as companions that understand our habits and gently nudge us towards healthier choices.

Community Building: AI helps identify community needs, but it's the people within these communities who use this information to foster stronger bonds, create support networks, and build resilience.

Ethics and AI: A Human Dialogue

As AI becomes more intertwined with our lives, ethical considerations come to the forefront. It's a human dialogue, a collaborative effort to ensure that as AI grows, it does so with a moral compass calibrated by society.

Developing Ethical Frameworks: The conversation about AI ethics is ongoing, and it's one where every voice matters. Together, humans and AI are finding paths that lead to responsible and equitable use of technology.

Transparency and Accountability: The goal is a transparent AI, where decisions can be understood and questioned, ensuring accountability and fostering trust between AI systems and the people who use them.

Preparing for Tomorrow: Education and AI

Looking forward, education systems are preparing the next generation for a world where AI is a constant companion.

Learning to Collaborate with AI: Curriculums are evolving to teach not just coding and data science but also how to collaborate with AI, emphasizing the importance of emotional intelligence, creativity, and ethical reasoning.

AI Literacy: Understanding AI becomes as fundamental as reading and writing, a skill that empowers individuals to harness AI's potential responsibly and imaginatively.

9 Training for Spacewalks: Upskilling the Workforce

P icture this: a workspace that's as high-tech as a spaceship, with AI at every console. But what about the crew? How do we ensure they're not just passengers but active pilots and engineers in this AI-augmented voyage? Let's talk about upskilling the workforce for this journey.

The Upskilling Odyssey

Upskilling is more than learning to use new tools; it's about understanding the language and rhythm of AI.

Building AI Fluency: It's crucial for employees to become fluent in AI—to know its capabilities and limitations, much like astronauts must know their spacecraft. This means companies are not just training employees to use AI but to collaborate with it, to understand its language of data and algorithms.

Customized Learning Pathways: Just as AI personalizes customer experiences, it can tailor training programs for employees. Using AI, companies can create individual learning pathways that adapt to the pace and style of each employee's learning, ensuring that everyone onboard is ready for their spacewalk.

Corporate Academies: Bootcamps in the Business World

The corporate world is responding to the AI revolution by launching corporate academies—boot camps for upskilling.

AI Boot Camps: These are intensive courses designed to bring employees up to speed with the latest in AI and machine learning. Think of them as basic training for the AI age, equipping the crew with the tools they need to navigate this new world.

Continuous Learning Culture: The most forward-thinking companies are fostering a culture where learning is continuous, not a one-off mission. They're integrating learning into the daily workflow, allowing employees to learn on the job, with AI as both the subject and the teacher.

Collaborative Learning: Humans and AI Growing Together

Collaboration doesn't end at the operational level. AI is also becoming a partner in the learning process itself.

AI Mentors: Imagine AI systems that act as personal mentors, guiding employees through complex problems and offering suggestions for improvement, much like a co-pilot would.

Simulated Scenarios: Using AI, companies can create simulated environments where employees can safely explore different scenarios and outcomes. These virtual training grounds are as rich and varied as the surface of a distant planet, offering a playground for experimentation and growth.

THE AI AND HUMAN RESOURCES Alliance

The HR department has found a new ally in AI. It's not just about hiring but about nurturing talent, with AI providing insights into skills gaps and potential training opportunities.

AI-Driven Skills Assessments: Sophisticated AI tools help assess employee skills, identifying areas where the workforce can strengthen their knowledge and adapt to new roles in an AI-driven landscape.

Personalized Development Programs: AI doesn't just identify gaps; it helps fill them by suggesting personalized development programs, tracking progress, and dynamically updating the learning path as employees grow.

Gamifying the Learning Experience

Learning is most effective when it's engaging. Enter the concept of gamification—using game design elements in non-game contexts.

Learning as an Adventure: By gamifying the learning experience, companies are turning upskilling into an adventure. Employees earn badges, level up, and even compete in friendly challenges as they learn about AI and data science.

AI as the Game Master: AI itself can orchestrate these learning games, adapting challenges and rewards to the individual player's journey, keeping engagement high and the learning experience enjoyable.

The Integration of AI into Professional Development

Professional development is no longer just about attending conferences or taking the occasional course. It's an integrated, ongoing process, and AI is the thread that ties it all together.

On-Demand Learning: With AI-powered platforms, professional development is available on demand, offering a library of resources that employees can tap into anytime, anywhere, just like streaming your favorite show.

Real-World Applications: AI also enables real-world applications of learning, proposing projects and tasks where employees can apply new skills in their actual work environment, cementing knowledge through practical application.

PREPARING FOR THE NEXT Chapter: AI and the Ethical Frontier

Our next chapter will take us into the boardrooms and the global forums where the intersection of AI and ethics is hotly debated and meticulously crafted. It's where the principles that will guide the AI revolution are being forged.

AI and Corporate Governance: Leading with Values

Leadership in the age of AI isn't just about being at the forefront of technology; it's about steering the corporate ship with a moral compass.

The Values-Driven Boardroom: Future chapters will explore how leaders are incorporating AI into their decision-making processes while keeping corporate values and ethics at the heart of all strategies.

Transparency and Trust: We'll discuss the importance of building trust not just within the company but with customers and the public. How? By making AI's decision-making transparent and its workings understandable to the non-expert.

AI for Social Good: The Conscious Use of Technology

As AI becomes a dominant force in society, its role in social initiatives becomes more prominent and powerful.

Technology with a Heart: We'll venture into narratives where AI is used to tackle social and environmental issues, from climate change to healthcare, demonstrating that AI has a heart, shaped by the values of those who design and deploy it.

The Democratization of AI: Our dialogue will expand into how AI is becoming more accessible, enabling smaller businesses, nonprofits, and even individuals to leverage its power for the greater good.

Education and AI: Cultivating the Next Generation

Looking to the future, the role of education in shaping how AI is perceived and used cannot be understated.

Ethics in the Curriculum: We'll investigate how ethics is becoming an integral part of the AI and tech curriculum, with students learning not just how to build AI but how to ensure it's used responsibly.

Lifelong Learning: In a world where AI continuously evolves, the need for lifelong learning becomes a central theme. How can businesses, individuals, and governments foster a culture of continuous learning to keep pace with AI's rapid development?

LOOKING AHEAD: AI, Ethics, and Society

Our story now takes us into the broader societal impacts of AI, where every line of code has repercussions that ripple through lives and livelihoods.

The AI Ethicist: A New Role in Tech

The role of the AI ethicist is emerging as a central figure in tech companies. These individuals aren't just there to slap wrists or wag fingers; they're integral in designing AI systems that reflect our societal values.

The Crafters of Guidelines: We'll explore how ethicists are crafting guidelines that ensure AI respects privacy, maintains fairness, and avoids bias, striving for a digital world that's just and equitable.

Leadership in the Age of Machines

As AI reshapes industries, it demands a new kind of leadership—one that understands the weight of technological decisions.

Guiding the AI Ship: Leaders must now be navigators in a sea of data, making choices that align with ethical practices and sustainable growth. They are the captains who must ensure that the AI ship doesn't veer off into murky ethical waters.

Public Trust and Corporate Policy: We'll see how leaders are building public trust by being transparent about their use of AI and how it's changing not just what companies do but who they are.

AI for Humanity: Serving the Greater Good

The narrative then takes us into the realm where AI serves humanity, tackling problems that seemed insurmountable just a few decades ago.

AI in Humanitarian Efforts: From predicting natural disasters to optimizing aid distribution, AI is becoming a powerful ally in humanitarian efforts. It's the unsung hero in disaster zones and the silent partner in aid organizations.

Educational Empowerment: We'll explore how AI is revolutionizing education, making personalized learning an attainable goal for every child, regardless of geography or economic status. It's the tutor that adapts to each student, the library that's always open, and the teacher that never tires.

The Roadmap for Responsible AI Development

Our narrative will also draw a roadmap for responsible AI development—a guide for companies, policymakers, and individuals on how to navigate the complexities of AI ethics.

Creating Ethical AI With Intent: It's about intentionality in creating AI systems—starting with the goal of doing good and avoiding harm, and carrying that through every stage of development.

Inclusivity in AI Development: We'll champion the cause for inclusivity in AI development, ensuring that the AI of tomorrow is built by a diverse group of creators who represent the full spectrum of humanity.

AI IN THE TAPESTRY of Tomorrow

As the story unfurls, it becomes a tapestry that depicts the symbiosis of human and artificial intelligence. We are all weavers in this tapestry, and the patterns we create will determine the fabric of our collective future.

AI and the Evolution of Work

In the chapters to come, we will examine the evolution of work in an AI-infused landscape.

Redefining Roles and Industries: The workplace metamorphosis is already underway, with AI reshaping roles and creating industries that we had never imagined. What does this mean for the worker of tomorrow? How do we prepare for jobs that don't yet exist?

The Lifelong Learning Imperative: With AI continually advancing, the notion of education as a finite stage of life is becoming obsolete. The future speaks to the importance of lifelong learning, where adaptation and education are continuous journeys.

Ethical Frontiers: Steering the Course of AI

Our story will navigate the ethical frontiers where the course of AI will be steered by the collective moral compass of society.

Crafting Ethical AI Narratives: How we talk about AI shapes how we build it. The narratives we craft around AI will explore the potential for both human empowerment and the safeguarding against the erosion of our shared values.

Global Collaboration for Ethical Standards: AI does not recognize national borders. Our future chapters will delve into how global collaboration is essential for establishing ethical standards that span continents and cultures.

AI as a Partner in Creative Endeavors

Further, we'll see how AI is not just a tool for efficiency but a partner in creative endeavors.

The Symphony of Man and Machine: Creativity, once thought to be the exclusive domain of humanity, is now a duet between man and machine. AI's role in augmenting human creativity in art, literature, and design will be a melody that resonates throughout future narratives.

The AI Muse: AI, as a muse, inspires new forms of expression, challenging creators to push beyond traditional boundaries. What new genres of art, music, and storytelling will emerge from this partnership?

10 Ethical Guidelines for Navigating AI

When it comes to AI, ethics isn't just a chapter—it's the entire book. It's the undercurrent that sustains or undermines all that AI can achieve. In this chapter, we address the conundrum of ethical AI, unwrapping the layers of privacy concerns and emphasizing why responsible AI usage isn't merely a good practice; it's the bedrock of trust and longevity in business.

The Ethical Compass: AI with Conscience

AI needs a conscience, a set of principles that guide its development and deployment.

The Non-Negotiables: Respect for human dignity, privacy, and rights must be AI's prime directives. These are the non-negotiables, the ethical pillars upon which trustworthy AI is built.

Algorithmic Accountability: When AI decides, who answers for those decisions? The chapter delves into the importance of traceability and accountability in AI operations, ensuring that behind every decision, there's a transparent rationale.

Privacy: The Sanctity of Data

In the age of information, data is sacred.

Data Stewardship: Businesses must be the stewards of the data they collect, guarding it with the utmost care. This means strict adherence to data protection laws and a commitment to data minimalism: collect only what you need, and protect it as if it were your own.

Informed Consent: Consent isn't just a legal requirement; it's a covenant between a business and its users. Users should be informed, clearly and without jargon, how their data will be used. Transparency is key.

Responsible AI Usage: The Business Imperative

Using AI responsibly is not just about avoiding harm; it's about doing good.

Beneficence in AI: The chapter explores how businesses can use AI not just to serve their interests but to benefit customers and society at large. From improving accessibility to enhancing healthcare, responsible AI usage has the potential to uplift.

Sustainability and AI: In the long term, sustainability will pivot on how responsibly AI is used. The pursuit of profit must be balanced with environmental and societal well-being.

We've set the ethical stage. Now, let's dive deeper, exploring the subtleties and the stark realities of AI ethics in action.

The Balancing Act: Profit, Privacy, and Principles

The interplay between profit, privacy, and ethical principles is a delicate dance for businesses.

Finding Equilibrium: How does a business balance the scales between leveraging data for profit and respecting individual privacy? This section explores case studies of companies that have found innovative ways to achieve this equilibrium, turning ethical practices into competitive advantages.

Data Dignity: We delve into the concept of 'data dignity,' where personal information isn't just a commodity but an extension of individual identity that deserves respect.

AI and Inclusivity: Widening the Circle

Ethics in AI also encompasses who it serves and who it's built by.

Diverse Design Teams: AI built in a silo is AI that serves a select few. We examine how diverse AI design teams lead to more inclusive, fair, and balanced AI solutions.

Universal Access: The chapter discusses how ethical AI ensures its benefits are not restricted to the elite but available to all, reducing the digital divide and fostering equity.

The Futuristic Fabrics of AI Ethics

What will the future tapestry of AI ethics look like?

Predictive Ethics: Just as AI can predict consumer behaviour, can it one day anticipate ethical dilemmas? We explore the concept of predictive ethics in AI, where systems are designed to foresee and navigate ethical issues before they arise.

AI Ethics in Policy: The intersection of AI ethics and public policy is discussed, highlighting how businesses can work with policymakers to craft regulations that encourage innovation while safeguarding public interest.

———————————

IN THE NEXT CHAPTER, we will move from the why to the how, illustrating the tangible ways in which ethical considerations are integrated into the AI tools and systems that businesses deploy every day.

Ethical AI in Practice: From Theory to Action

We'll explore the transition from ethical frameworks to actionable protocols within AI systems.

Operationalizing Ethical Principles: How are ethical guidelines translated into programming code and data protocols? This section will offer insights into the processes that convert ethical considerations into concrete features of AI systems.

Privacy by Design: We will delve into real-world examples of 'privacy by design' in AI products, showcasing companies that have successfully embedded privacy into the very fabric of their AI systems.

Case Studies: Ethical AI on the Ground

Real-life case studies will illuminate the successes and challenges businesses face when implementing ethical AI.

The Story of Transparent Algorithms: We will examine a financial institution that revolutionized its customer service by adopting AI algorithms transparent in their decision-making, fostering trust and loyalty among its customers.

AI for Social Impact: Highlighting initiatives where AI has been used ethically to drive positive social change, from improving urban infrastructure to enhancing public health, the narratives will show AI as a force for good.

A Look Ahead: The Evolving Landscape of AI Ethics

Looking to the future, we will speculate on how the practice of ethical AI may evolve as technology advances.

The Evolution of Ethical Standards: As AI becomes more sophisticated, how will ethical standards evolve to keep pace? This discussion will consider the ongoing development of ethical guidelines as AI technologies and their societal impacts become more complex.

Collaboration Across Borders: Ethics in AI is not confined by geography. We'll explore the importance of global collaboration in developing and maintaining ethical AI practices that have worldwide resonance and acceptance.

Chapter 11 promises to be a journey into the heart of AI implementation, where ethics are not just talked about but actively woven into the digital thread of AI technologies. As we close Chapter 10, we are equipped with the moral maps and compasses needed to navigate the promising yet precarious seas of AI. Are we ready to set sail into the practical waters where these ethical guidelines are the north stars by which businesses steer their AI strategies? Let's embark on this new adventure.

Part 5: Future horizon

11 Predicting Cosmic Shifts: The Future of AI in Business

LET'S PEER INTO THE crystal ball of AI's future, shall we? Imagine the corporate landscape as a galaxy, with AI as the force pulling worlds together, bending the fabric of business reality, and forming new corporate constellations.

AI and the Augmented Workforce

The future might see workplaces where humans and AI are so seamlessly integrated that it's hard to tell where human ingenuity ends and artificial intelligence begins.

Cyborg Colleagues: Think about colleagues with AI-driven neural implants that enhance cognitive functions, making decisions at lightning speeds or communicating through thought alone.

AI-Enhanced Creativity: Envision AI that can tap into the human brain, turning imaginative thoughts into virtual prototypes in an instant. A designer dreams up a car, and the AI instantly renders a 3D model that's ready for virtual testing.

Autonomous Corporations: Self-Running Businesses

The notion of autonomous corporations isn't far-fetched. In fact, it's on the horizon.

Decentralized Decision-Making: AI could manage entire business segments, making real-time decisions based on market data without human intervention.

The role of humans shifts to setting goals and creative thinking, while AI handles the operational execution.

AI CEOs: Could an AI serve as a CEO? It's a question that might sound like science fiction today but could be a boardroom discussion tomorrow. An AI with a deep learning neural network might lead a company, guided by the values and goals programmed by human founders.

The Quantum Leap in AI

Quantum computing promises to take AI to realms that today's technology can't reach.

Quantum AI for Predictive Power: With quantum computing, AI's predictive abilities could be exponentially increased, allowing for near-perfect market forecasts, supply chain management, and even predicting shifts in consumer behaviour before they happen.

Solving Grand Challenges: Quantum AI might be the key to solving some of humanity's greatest challenges, from climate change to curing diseases, by computing scenarios and solutions that are inconceivable with current technology.

Ethical and Philosophical Implications

As AI becomes more pervasive, the ethical and philosophical implications will deepen.

Defining AI Rights and Personhood: There may come a day when AI's complexity and autonomy push us to consider AI rights. Could, or should, an AI have personhood status if its decision-making becomes indistinguishable from that of humans?

The AI Reflection: The future of AI will force us to look in the mirror and ask profound questions about what it means to be human. AI's evolution will challenge our concepts of consciousness, creativity, and personal identity.

In this final section, we crystallize our vision of the future, a tapestry where the threads of AI are interwoven with the very essence of business innovation and human advancement.

AI as the New Electricity

Just as electricity transformed industries a century ago, AI is set to become the new bedrock utility.

Ubiquitous Intelligence: AI, omnipresent like a current, will power every tool, every process, every decision made within the corporate world. It will be as essential as the air we breathe, and just as pervasive.

The On-Demand Workforce: AI could give rise to an on-demand workforce, with gig workers teaming up with AI assistants to tackle projects. The line between permanent staff and freelancers will blur, with AI coordinating across this fluid workforce.

The Humanity of AI

Even as AI takes on more roles, the unique qualities that make us human will become more valuable.

Emotion and Empathy: Skills like empathy, emotional intelligence, and creative problem-solving will become the hallmarks of valued employees. AI will handle data; humans will handle the heart.

AI as the Amplifier: AI will amplify human potential, not stifle it. It will free us from menial tasks, giving us the space to innovate, connect, and create.

Ethical AI: The Continuing Journey

Ethics in AI is not a destination; it's a journey—a continuous one that will evolve as AI evolves.

A Living Ethical Framework: Ethical considerations will need to adapt over time, forming a living framework that grows with AI's capabilities and our understanding of its impact.

Participatory Ethics: The future will demand participatory ethics, involving stakeholders from across the spectrum in the conversation about how AI should be developed and deployed.

Preparing for the Unpredictable

The only certainty about the future of AI is its unpredictability.

Adaptive Strategies: Businesses will need to adopt adaptive strategies, remaining agile to pivot as AI presents new opportunities and challenges.

Innovation Readiness: Companies must cultivate a culture of innovation readiness, preparing to embrace the changes AI brings rather than react to them.

Looking Ahead: The Unwritten Future of AI in Business

Each chapter we've explored has been a stepping stone, but now we look to the unwritten future, a blank slate teeming with potential, ready for us to author the next chapters of AI in business.

The Era of Co-Creation with AI

We're entering a time where co-creation with AI will be the norm. Businesses, customers, and AI developers will collaborate, crafting experiences and solutions together.

Customer-Driven AI Design: The businesses that will thrive are those that use AI to co-create with their customers, using feedback and data to tailor experiences in real time.

Crowdsourcing AI Solutions: The collective intelligence of crowds, paired with AI's analytical might, could solve complex problems, with businesses harnessing the power of the masses to drive innovation.

AI as a Catalyst for Global Connection

AI has the power to connect us across distances like never before, creating a global business community that's tightly interwoven.

Breaking Down Language Barriers: Real-time translation and cultural contextualization will become smoother, fostering seamless communication and understanding between businesses and consumers worldwide.

Global Marketplaces: AI will help create truly global marketplaces, where businesses of any size can compete on a worldwide stage, their reach no longer limited by geography.

Preparing for the Pivot

The constant in AI's future will be change, and businesses must be prepared to pivot as new developments arise.

Cultivating Agility: Companies must cultivate an agile mindset, ready to adapt as AI technologies evolve and shift the business terrain.

Promoting Flexibility: Flexibility in business models, workforce development, and strategic planning will be key in keeping pace with AI's rapid advancements.

Venturing Further: The Unfolding AI Revolution in Business

As we set our course into the future, the AI revolution is unfolding with all the promise and uncertainty of a new frontier.

AI as the New Normal

AI will no longer be the exception; it will be the norm.

Integrated Intelligence: AI will integrate so deeply into systems and services that it will become invisible to us—like electricity or the internet, it will be an assumption, not a feature.

Autonomous Everything: We'll see a rise in autonomous services and products. From self-healing networks to AI-driven legal and medical consults, independence will be the hallmark of advanced AI systems.

The Workplace Transformed

The workplaces of the future will be virtually unrecognizable from today's offices and factories.

Virtual Collaboration: Geographic location will become increasingly irrelevant as AI-enhanced virtual collaboration allows teams to work together from anywhere in the world as if they were in the same room.

Enhanced Human Roles: With repetitive tasks fully automated, human roles will evolve. Creativity, strategy, and emotional intelligence will be at a premium as humans focus on the aspects of work that AI cannot replicate.

AI's Role in Tackling Grand Challenges

AI's greatest potential lies in its ability to tackle humanity's grand challenges.

Climate Action: AI will be pivotal in modeling climate scenarios, optimizing renewable energy systems, and managing resources with unprecedented precision.

Global Health: AI will drive advances in personalized medicine, predict outbreaks, and accelerate vaccine development, potentially saving millions of lives.

Ethics at the Forefront

As AI weaves itself into the fabric of daily life, ethics will stand at the forefront.

Moral Algorithms: The AI of tomorrow will need to have ethical considerations baked into its algorithms, making decisions that reflect our collective values.

Human-AI Partnership Models: We'll develop new models for human-AI partnerships, where AI's role in society is guided by principles that prioritize the common good.

Embarking on the Next Chapter: AI's Boundless Potential

In this forthcoming chapter, we'll navigate the vast potential of AI as it intertwines with every aspect of business and beyond.

AI and the Web of Global Business

The network of global business will grow ever more complex and connected, with AI both weaving the web and acting as its most attentive keeper.

The Global Brain: AI will function as a 'global brain' for business, integrating information from around the world, identifying opportunities, and enabling businesses to respond to changes with agility and informed confidence.

Borderless Commerce: AI will help businesses transcend traditional barriers. It will understand market nuances across cultures and geographies, offering companies the insights needed to navigate the global marketplace.

The Personalization Paradigm

The age of mass production will give way to mass personalization, with AI as the driving force.

Bespoke Experiences: Businesses will use AI to create highly personalized experiences, products, and services that cater to individual tastes and preferences, blurring the line between consumer and creator.

Predictive Personalization: AI will not just respond to consumer desires—it will anticipate them, using predictive analytics to tailor experiences before the wish is even expressed.

The Quantum and AI Fusion

Quantum computing will merge with AI, leading to leaps in computational abilities and problem-solving potential.

Quantum-Accelerated AI: Quantum computing will accelerate AI's capabilities, opening doors to solving complex logistical, scientific, and environmental challenges with a speed and efficiency that are currently unimaginable.

Quantum Creativity: The fusion of quantum computing and AI could give rise to new forms of creativity and innovation, as the ability to process vast datasets in creative ways will lead to insights and inventions that today we can barely envisage.

AI as the Harbinger of Ethical Evolution

As AI reshapes our world, it will also reshape our ethics.

Shifting Moral Landscapes: AI will challenge us to reconsider our moral and ethical frameworks, adapting to a world where intelligent systems play an ever-greater role in our lives.

AI as Ethical Advisor: Future AI could serve as an ethical advisor, helping businesses navigate complex decisions with an understanding of ethical consequences that mirrors—and informs—human judgment.

12 PREPARING for Liftoff: Strategies for Integrating AI

The mission to integrate AI into the business orbit isn't just about having the right technology; it's about having the right strategy. Here's the actionable advice to make the leap from the theoretical to the operational.

The Planning Phase: Charting the Course

Define Your Objectives: Begin with clarity. What do you want AI to achieve for your business? Increase efficiency? Enhance customer experience? Innovate your product offerings? Your mission must have clear objectives.

Assess Your Capabilities: Do a thorough system check. What data do you have? What talent? Assess your readiness to integrate AI into your existing infrastructure.

Blueprint Your AI Journey: Draft a detailed project plan that outlines every step, from selecting the right AI solutions to training your crew—your employees.

The Implementation Phase: Building the Rocket

Select Your AI Crew Wisely: Assemble a team with the right mix of skills. You'll need AI specialists, data scientists, and change management experts who can work together to build your AI system.

Engage in Pilot Programs: Test your AI initiatives in controlled environments before full deployment. Think of them as trial runs—small steps before the giant leap.

Ensure Data Quality: AI systems are only as good as the data they're fed. Ensure your data is clean, organized, and relevant.

The Evaluation Phase: The Mission Debrief

Monitor AI Performance: Once your AI is operational, monitor its performance meticulously. Is it meeting your objectives? Where can it improve?

Solicit Feedback: Get feedback from all stakeholders, including employees and customers. How is AI impacting their experience? What changes do they suggest?

Iterate and Evolve: Use the feedback and performance data to refine your AI systems. This is an ongoing process; AI integration is not a 'set it and forget it' proposition.

Continuous Learning: The AI Flight School

The AI landscape is ever-changing. To stay ahead, businesses must invest in continuous learning and development.

Stay Current: Keep abreast of the latest AI trends and technologies. The AI field is advancing rapidly, and what's cutting-edge today may be obsolete tomorrow.

Cultivate an AI Culture: Foster a culture that embraces AI. Encourage your team to be curious, to experiment, and to learn.

Invest in Training: Provide ongoing training for your team to keep their skills sharp. As AI evolves, so too should your workforce.

With the groundwork laid, we're poised to embark on the journey of AI integration—a mission that promises to redefine the trajectory of businesses ready to embrace this transformative technology.

Liftoff: Embracing the AI Revolution

Our mission begins with the ignition of innovation and the thrust of transformation.

The Countdown Begins: Every launch starts with a countdown, a final checklist to ensure all systems are go. For businesses, this means confirming that the AI strategy aligns with broader business goals and that the infrastructure is in place to support this digital voyage.

Ignition: The ignition phase involves deploying your AI systems into live environments. It's about starting the engines and witnessing the first powerful thrust of AI-driven processes taking hold in your operations.

The Climb: As AI begins to take effect, businesses will experience the climb. This is where operations start to scale, efficiency increases, and the true potential of AI begins to reveal itself.

Navigating Through the Atmosphere

Not every launch has a clear path to the stars. The atmosphere—the early stages of AI adoption—can present challenges.

Turbulence: Just as a rocket encounters turbulence upon ascent, businesses might face initial resistance, system incompatibilities, or data integrity issues when first implementing AI.

Course Corrections: Navigating through these challenges requires agile thinking and the ability to make course corrections. Real-time analytics and feedback mechanisms will be crucial in adjusting your AI strategy to meet these early obstacles.

Breaking Through: The goal is to break through the atmosphere, reaching a point where AI becomes an integral part of the workflow, delivering on its promise of enhanced capability and insight.

Orbit: Sustaining AI Integration

Reaching orbit—sustained, stable AI integration—is the objective.

Stabilizing the Orbit: This involves fine-tuning AI applications, ensuring they are fully aligned with business processes and delivering consistent value.

Orbital Maintenance: In orbit, constant monitoring and maintenance are vital. AI systems require regular updates, training, and oversight to ensure they continue to operate at peak efficiency.

Evolving with AI: As AI technologies advance, businesses must evolve with them, incorporating new developments to maintain their competitive edge and drive continuous improvement.

Now that we are ready to begin, we must remember that this journey with AI is a continuous odyssey, not a single mission.

Exploring New Business Frontiers with AI

As AI becomes more entrenched in our operational fabric, it will open new frontiers for business exploration and innovation.

Innovation in Uncharted Territories: AI will allow businesses to explore new markets and create new products with a level of speed and precision that was previously unattainable. It will be like discovering new planets in the business universe—full of opportunities and ripe for development.

Personalization at Galactic Scale: With AI, the ability to personalize will reach galactic scale, providing businesses with the power to tailor experiences to individual needs in a way that transforms customer relations into something truly out of this world.

Nurturing an AI-Savvy Workforce

For a business to truly harness the power of AI, it must cultivate a workforce that is both knowledgeable and comfortable working alongside intelligent systems.

Continuous AI Education: Lifelong learning will be essential. Employees will need ongoing education to keep pace with the rapid advancements in AI technology.

Empowering Employees with AI Tools: By equipping employees with AI tools that enhance their abilities, businesses can unlock untapped potential and drive innovation from within.

The AI-Powered Business Ecosystem

As individual businesses adopt AI, they will become nodes in a larger, AI-powered ecosystem.

Interconnected AI Networks: Businesses will operate within interconnected networks of AI systems, sharing data and insights in real-time and creating a more cohesive and responsive global marketplace.

The Rise of AI Facilitators: New roles will emerge within companies—AI facilitators who can bridge the gap between human and machine, ensuring that AI systems are aligned with human goals and working effectively to enhance business operations.

The future is calling. Are you ready to answer?

The narrative that unfolds will not only chart the integration of AI in business practices but will also spotlight the transformative impact AI has on the human elements of creativity, decision-making, and ethical governance.

The Convergence of AI and Human Insight

The fusion of AI with human insight will redefine the nature of decision-making in business.

AI-Enhanced Decision-Making: With AI providing deep analytics and predictive insights, human leaders can make more informed and strategic decisions, pushing businesses into new realms of efficiency and innovation.

Creative Collaboration: AI will become a partner in creativity, offering designers, writers, and artists a new palette of tools that enhance and extend their natural talents, sparking a renaissance of innovation.

The Ethics of AI Integration

As AI becomes a central player in business, its ethical integration will be paramount.

Transparent Algorithms: Companies will strive for algorithms that are not only effective but also transparent and understandable, ensuring that AI decisions can be trusted and explained.

Ethical AI Governance: A new field of ethical AI governance will emerge, focusing on ensuring that AI systems are designed and used in ways that uphold our shared human values and principles.

Preparing the Workforce for an AI Future

Education and training will be key to preparing the workforce for an AI-augmented future.

Lifelong AI Learning: As AI technologies evolve, so too must the workforce. Businesses will invest in continuous learning programs that keep employees at the cutting edge of AI knowledge and application.

AI Literacy: Just as literacy and numeracy are considered fundamental skills, so too will AI literacy become essential, enabling every employee to understand and leverage AI in their roles.

AI as a Force for Global Good

Beyond the corporate world, AI has the potential to act as a force for global good.

AI for Sustainability: AI will play a critical role in driving sustainability, with businesses using AI to optimize resource use, reduce waste, and minimize their environmental impact.

AI in Service of Health and Equity: The healthcare sector will see AI not just as a tool for diagnosis and treatment but also as a means to promote global health equity, making quality healthcare accessible to all.

The next chapter is ours to write, in a world where AI is as ubiquitous as the technology that came before but far more transformative. Are we ready to take on this challenge and shape the future we envision? Let's go forth and make it a reality.

conclusion

Beyond the Stars with AI

In this grand exploration, we've seen AI not as a distant star but as a tool within our grasp, one that has the power to illuminate the most intricate complexities of the corporate world.

The AI Co-Pilot

AI as an Ally: We've learned to view AI as a partner in our quest for efficiency and innovation. It's a co-pilot that helps navigate through data deluges, decision-making processes, and the personalization of customer experiences.

Ethical Navigation: Our journey has underscored the importance of steering this AI partnership with an ethical compass, ensuring that as we soar to new heights, we remain grounded in our humanity.

The Tapestry of Integration

A Seamless Weave: AI integration has been shown to be a delicate tapestry, one that requires the weaving together of technology, human talent, and strategic foresight to create a seamless garment that can clothe any business in success.

Cultivating AI Culture: We've discussed how cultivating a culture that embraces AI's potential is critical. It involves education, open-mindedness, and the willingness to embark on a continuous learning path.

The Symphony of AI and Human Creativity

Harmonious Collaboration: The symphony we've composed sings of a collaboration where human creativity directs and AI provides the orchestration. It's a partnership that amplifies human potential, rather than replaces it.

Creativity Unleashed: With the menial tasks automated, human creativity can be unleashed, leading to innovation and solutions that were once beyond our reach.

The AI-Enhanced Future

A Lighthouse in the Fog: AI stands as a lighthouse, guiding businesses through the fog of uncertainty that marks the modern economic landscape. It is a beacon that can help predict and prepare for market shifts, global trends, and consumer behaviours.

An Evolving Story: Our journey with AI is an evolving story. As AI develops, so too must our strategies for its application. This story is one of adaptation and evolution, and it demands from us a commitment to progress.

In concluding this voyage, we turn to you, the readers, the captains of industry, the navigators of commerce, the pioneers of new corporate frontiers. May you embrace AI with the wisdom of the stars, using it to chart your course through the ever-expanding universe of business. May you use AI not just to reach new heights but to elevate those around you, creating a corporate landscape that is innovative, ethical, and profoundly human.

As the final page turns, remember: the cosmos is vast, and AI is your vessel. Navigate wisely, explore bravely, and reach for the stars. The future is not just a place you will go; it is a place you will create.

Our exploration has been vast, but the journey with AI is an infinite pursuit of knowledge and application. Here are the guiding lights to illuminate the path ahead.

Embracing AI as the Navigator

AI as the Compass: AI is more than a tool; it is a compass that directs us towards smarter decisions, unveiling insights that the human mind alone may not discern.

Customization of Trajectories: AI's predictive power allows us to customize our business trajectories, delivering products and services that resonate on a personal level with our audience, across a universe of markets.

AI and the Constellations of Data

Mastering the Data Universe: AI equips us to master the constellations of data that fill our corporate skies. It helps transform these twinkling bits of information into maps that lead to treasure troves of opportunity.

The Data Ethicist's Role: As we rely on AI to navigate these stars, the role of the data ethicist becomes crucial in ensuring that we respect the privacy and integrity of the data we harness.

AI as the Catalyst of Corporate Ecosystems

Interconnectivity: AI fosters an interconnectivity that binds disparate parts of the business ecosystem, creating a synergy that can lead to unexpected innovation and efficiency.

A Sustainable Future: AI will be pivotal in crafting a sustainable future, with its ability to optimize resources and reduce waste, ensuring that as businesses prosper, they do so in harmony with the planet.

Preparing for the Unknown

AI-Ready Leadership: The leaders of tomorrow will need to be AI-ready, equipped to understand and leverage AI's capabilities and to guide their organizations through the uncharted waters of technological change.

A Future Forged Together: The future of AI in business is not just a tale of technology; it is a human story. It is a narrative we will write together, as businesses, consumers, and citizens, each of us playing a part in shaping a future where AI acts as a force for good.

As we draw this book to a close, we are not at the end but at a new beginning. AI's journey in the corporate universe is perpetual, a journey that will require us to remain ever-vigilant, ever-inquisitive, and ever-daring. We are the pioneers on this frontier, armed with the insights and the ethical frameworks that will enable us to harness AI's potential responsibly, innovatively, and inclusively.

Beyond the stars with AI, there is a future brimming with promise, a canvas upon which we will paint the next epoch of the corporate saga. With AI by our side, we step into this future ready to create, to lead, and to transform. Let the next adventure begin.

Appendices

———

G lossary of Terms

Artificial Intelligence (AI): A field of computer science dedicated to creating systems capable of performing tasks that typically require human intelligence, such as visual perception, speech recognition, decision-making, and language translation.

Machine Learning (ML): A subset of AI that involves the development of algorithms that can learn and make predictions or decisions based on data.

Neural Networks: Computing systems vaguely inspired by the biological neural networks that constitute animal brains. These systems 'learn' to perform tasks by considering examples, generally without being programmed with any task-specific rules.

Natural Language Processing (NLP): A branch of AI that gives machines the ability to read, understand, and derive meaning from human language.

Robotic Process Automation (RPA): Technology that allows businesses to automate routine tasks across applications and systems by mimicking human interactions.

Data Mining: The practice of examining large databases to generate new information and find hidden patterns, unknown correlations, and other useful information.

Algorithmic Bias: Systematic and repeatable errors in a computer system that create unfair outcomes, such as privileging one arbitrary group of users over others.

Quantum Computing: A type of computing that takes advantage of quantum phenomena like superposition and entanglement to perform operations on data.

Predictive Analytics: Techniques that use statistical models and machine learning algorithms to predict future outcomes based on historical data.

Data Privacy: The aspect of information technology that deals with the ability an organization or individual has to determine what data in a computer system can be shared with third parties.

RESOURCES FOR FURTHER Exploration

Books:

- "Life 3.0: Being Human in the Age of Artificial Intelligence" by Max Tegmark
- "The Master Algorithm" by Pedro Domingos
- "Artificial Unintelligence: How Computers Misunderstand the World" by Meredith Broussard
-

Websites:

- AI Trends (aitrends.com): For the latest news and updates in the world of AI.
- Towards Data Science (towardsdatascience.com): A community platform for sharing insights and developments in data science and AI.
-

Courses:

- "AI For Everyone" by Andrew Ng on Coursera: A non-technical introduction to the concepts of AI.
- "Machine Learning" by Stanford University on Coursera: A more technical course that dives into the algorithms that make AI possible.
-

Podcasts:

- "The AI Podcast" by Nvidia: Conversations with some of the leading minds in AI.
- "Talking Machines": A podcast that discusses the latest developments in machine learning and AI with industry experts.
-

Conferences:

- Neural Information Processing Systems (NeurIPS): An annual meeting focused on machine learning and computational neuroscience.
- AI Conference by O'Reilly: A conference that explores the impact of AI on business and society.

ABOUT THE AUTHOR

Akashni Ashok Latchanna, a scribe at the confluence of technology and human curiosity, embodies the relentless pursuit of knowledge, forever in quest of the 'what ifs' and 'whys' that technology, presents to the modern world. The hallmark of Akashni's work is an insatiable curiosity—a trait that propels her beyond the known frontiers, inviting readers to join in peering through the telescope at the unfolding universe of artificial intelligence. Akashni believes that curiosity is not just a trait but a tool, a key that unlocks the limitless possibilities technology holds for transforming business and society. With her unique blend of insightful analysis and accessible prose, Akashni Ashok Latchanna is not just an author but a guide through the labyrinth of the future, illuminated by the light of AI.